Slavoj Žižek is no ordinary thinker. Combining psychoanalysis, philosophy and politics into a compelling whole, Žižek's approach is always both fresh and fascinating. The scope of his subject matter is equally exhilarating, ranging from the political apathy of contemporary life, to a joke about the man who thinks he will be eaten by a chicken, from the ethical heroism of Keanu Reeves in 'Speed', to what toilet designs reveal about the national psyche. In this volume, Tony Myers provides a clear and engaging guide to Žižek's key ideas, explaining the main influences on Žižek's thought, including his crucial engagement with Lacanian psychoanalysis. Using examples drawn from popular culture and everyday life, Myers outlines for the first time the main issues that Žižek's work tackles, including:

- What is a subject and why is it so important?
- What is so terrible about postmodernity?
- How can we distinguish reality from ideology?
- What is the relationship between men and women?
- Why is racism always a fantasy?

Slavoj Žižek is essential reading for anyone wanting to understand the thought of the critic whom Terry Eagleton has described as 'the most formidably brilliant exponent of psychoanalysis, indeed of cultural theory in general, to have emerged in Europe for some decades'.

Tony Myers is a former lecturer at the University of Stirling. He is the author of *Upgrade Your English Essay* (Arnold 2002) and numerous articles on postmodernism, psychoanalysis and politics.

ROUTLEDGE CRITICAL THINKERS
essential guides for literary studies

Series Editor: Robert Eaglestone, Royal Holloway, University of London

Routledge Critical Thinkers is a series of accessible introductions to key figures in contemporary critical thought.

With a unique focus on historical and intellectual contexts, each volume examines a key theorist's:

- significance
- motivation
- key ideas and their sources
- impact on other thinkers

Concluding with extensively annotated guides to further reading, *Routledge Critical Thinkers* are the literature student's passport to today's most exciting critical thought.

Already available:
Jean Baudrillard by Richard J. Lane
Maurice Blanchot by Ullrich Haase and William Large
Judith Butler by Sara Salih
Gilles Deleuze by Claire Colebrook
Jacques Derrida by Nicholas Royle
Michel Foucault by Sara Mills
Sigmund Freud by Pamela Thurschwell
Stuart Hall by James Proctor
Martin Heidegger by Timothy Clark
Fredric Jameson by Adam Roberts
Jean-François Lyotard by Simon Malpas
Paul de Man by Martin McQuillan
Paul Ricoeur by Karl Simms
Edward Said by Bill Ashcroft and Pal Ahluwalia
Gayatri Chakravorty Spivak by Stephen Morton
Slavoj Žižek by Tony Myers

For further details on this series, see www.literature.routledge.com/rct

SLAVOJ ŽIŽEK

Tony Myers

LONDON AND NEW YORK

First published 2003
by Routledge
11 New Fetter Lane, London EC4P 4EE

Simultaneously published in the USA and Canada
by Routledge
29 West 35th Street, New York, NY 10001

Routledge is an imprint of the Taylor & Francis Group

© 2003 Tony Myers

Typeset in Perpetua by
Florence Production Ltd, Stoodleigh, Devon
Printed and bound in Great Britain by
TJ International Ltd, Padstow, Cornwall

British Library Cataloguing in Publication Data
A catalogue record for this book is available from the British Library

Library of Congress Cataloging in Publication Data
Myers, Tony, 1969–
Slavoj Žižek/Tony Myers. – 1st ed.
    p. cm. – (Routledge critical thinkers)
  Includes bibliographical references and index.
  1. Žižek, Slavoj. I. Title. II. Series.
  B4870.Z594M94 2003
  199'.4973–dc21   2003004342

ISBN 0–415–26264–X (hbk)
ISBN 0–415–26265–8 (pbk)

CONTENTS

SERIES EDITOR'S PREFACE

The books in this series offer introductions to major critical thinkers who have influenced literary studies and the humanities. The *Routledge Critical Thinkers* series provides the books you can turn to first when a new name or concept appears in your studies.

Each book will equip you to approach a key thinker's original texts by explaining her or his key ideas, putting them into context and, perhaps most importantly, showing you why this thinker is considered to be significant. The emphasis is on concise, clearly written guides which do not presuppose a specialist knowledge. Although the focus is on particular figures, the series stresses that no critical thinker ever existed in a vacuum but, instead, emerged from a broader intellectual, cultural and social history. Finally, these books will act as a bridge between you and the thinker's original texts: not replacing them but rather complementing what she or he wrote.

These books are necessary for a number of reasons. In his 1997 autobiography, *Not Entitled*, the literary critic Frank Kermode wrote of a time in the 1960s:

> On beautiful summer lawns, young people lay together all night, recovering from their daytime exertions and listening to a troupe of Balinese musicians. Under their blankets or their sleeping bags, they would chat drowsily about the gurus of the time. . . . What they repeated was largely hearsay; hence my

lunchtime suggestion, quite impromptu, for a series of short, very cheap books offering authoritative but intelligible introductions to such figures.

There is still a need for 'authoritative and intelligible introductions'. But this series reflects a different world from the 1960s. New thinkers have emerged and the reputations of others have risen and fallen, as new research has developed. New methodologies and challenging ideas have spread through the arts and humanities. The study of literature is no longer – if it ever was – simply the study and evaluation of poems, novels and plays. It is also the study of the ideas, issues and difficulties which arise in any literary text and in its interpretation. Other arts and humanities subjects have changed in analogous ways.

With these changes, new problems have emerged. The ideas and issues behind these radical changes in the humanities are often presented without reference to wider contexts or as theories which you can simply 'add on' to the texts you read. Certainly, there's nothing wrong with picking out selected ideas or using what comes to hand – indeed, some thinkers have argued that this is, in fact, all we can do. However, it is sometimes forgotten that each new idea comes from the pattern and development of somebody's thought and it is important to study the range and context of their ideas. Against theories 'floating in space', the *Routledge Critical Thinkers* series places key thinkers and their ideas firmly back in their contexts.

More than this, these books reflect the need to go back to the thinker's own texts and ideas. Every interpretation of an idea, even the most seemingly innocent one, offers its own 'spin', implicitly or explicitly. To read only books on a thinker, rather than texts by that thinker, is to deny yourself a chance of making up your own mind. Sometimes what makes a significant figure's work hard to approach is not so much its style or content as the feeling of not knowing where to start. The purpose of these books is to give you a 'way in' by offering an accessible overview of a these thinkers' ideas and works and by guiding your further reading, starting with each thinker's own texts. To use a metaphor from the philosopher Ludwig Wittgenstein (1889–1951), these books are ladders, to be thrown away after you have climbed to the next level. Not only, then, do they equip you to approach new ideas, but also they empower you, by leading you back to a theorist's own texts and encouraging you to develop your own informed opinions.

Finally, these books are necessary because, just as intellectual needs have changed, the education systems around the world – the contexts in which introductory books are usually read – have changed radically, too. What was suitable for the minority higher education system of the 1960s is not suitable for the larger, wider, more diverse, high technology education systems of the twenty-first century. These changes call not just for new, up-to-date, introductions but new methods of presentation. The presentational aspects of *Routledge Critical Thinkers* have been developed with today's students in mind.

Each book in the series has a similar structure. They begin with a section offering an overview of the life and ideas of each thinker and explain why she or he is important. The central section of each book discusses the thinker's key ideas, their context, evolution and reception. Each book concludes with a survey of the thinker's impact, outlining how their ideas have been taken up and developed by others. In addition, there is a detailed final section suggesting and describing books for further reading. This is not a 'tacked-on' section but an integral part of each volume. In the first part of this section you will find brief descriptions of the thinker's key works, then, following this, information on the most useful critical works and, in some cases, on relevant web sites. This section will guide you in your reading, enabling you to follow your interests and develop your own projects. Throughout each book, references are given in what is known as the Harvard system (the author and the date of a work cited are given in the text and you can look up the full details in the bibliography at the back). This offers a lot of information in very little space. The books also explain technical terms and use boxes to describe events or ideas in more detail, away from the main emphasis of the discussion. Boxes are also used at times to highlight definitions of terms frequently used or coined by a thinker. In this way, the boxes serve as a kind of glossary, easily identified when flicking through the book.

The thinkers in the series are 'critical' for three reasons. First, they are examined in the light of subjects which involve criticism: principally literary studies or English and cultural studies, but also other disciplines which rely on the criticism of books, ideas, theories and unquestioned assumptions. Second, studying their work will provide you with a 'tool kit' for informed critical reading and thought, which will heighten your own criticism. Third, these thinkers are critical because they are crucially important: they deal with ideas and questions which can overturn conventional understandings of the world, of texts, of everything we take for granted, leaving us with a deeper understanding of what we already knew and with new ideas.

No introduction can tell you everything. However, by offering a way into critical thinking, this series hopes to begin to engage you in an activity which is productive, constructive and potentially life-changing.

ACKNOWLEDGEMENTS

My first thanks go to Bob Eaglestone and Rebecca Barden for all their editorial chastening and championing during the lifetime of this book. I also owe a debt of gratitude to the generosity of Vance Adair, Malcolm Bowie, John Drakakis, Terry Hawkes, David Punter and Pat Waugh for their encouragement. Finally, I would like to record my unsurpassed appreciation to Ali for all her support.

ABBREVIATIONS

The following list contains the abbreviations used throughout the book which refer to Žižek's works. A more detailed bibliography can be found in the Further Reading section.

TMOE   *The Metastases of Enjoyment: Six Essays on Woman and Causality*
TPOF   *The Plague of Fantasies*
TTS   *The Ticklish Subject: The Absent Centre of Political Ontology*
TWTN   *Tarrying with the Negative: Kant, Hegel and the Critique of Ideology*
TZR   *The Žižek Reader*

WHY ŽIŽEK?

Slavoj Žižek is a philosopher. He is, however, no ordinary philosopher, for he thinks and writes in such a recklessly entertaining fashion, he constantly risks making philosophy enjoyable. With a happy disregard for the typically cloistered atmosphere of critical thought, Žižek's approach is frenetic and explosive. Swivelling on his heels, he berates the political apathy of contemporary life in one moment, jokes about the man who thinks he will be eaten by a chicken in the next, then explains the ethical heroism of Keanu Reeves in *Speed*, exposes the philosophical basis of Viagra, and finishes up with a disclosure of the paradoxical value of Christianity to Marxism. In doing so, Žižek takes psychoanalysis and philosophy by the scruff of their necks and forces them to confront everyday life. All of which has compelled the British critic Terry Eagleton (b. 1943) to describe Žižek 'as the most formidably brilliant exponent of psychoanalysis, indeed of cultural theory in general, to have emerged in Europe for some decades' (Eagleton 1997: 4).

The foundation of Žižek's 'formidable brilliance' is his amazement. For Slavoj Žižek is amazed. In fact, he is constantly amazed: *why*, he wonders, is everything like *that*? Of course, Žižek's amazement is a ruse. It is, however, a necessary ruse. For it is a form of quizzical vigilance which, he argues, constitutes the basis of critical thought itself: 'philosophy begins', Žižek contends, 'the moment we do not simply accept what exists as given ("It's like that!", "Law is law!", etc.), but

raise the question of how is what we encounter as actual also possible'
(*TWTN*: 2). With all the guile of a child asking his parents why the sky
is blue, Žižek questions everything that passes for wisdom about who
we are, what we are doing and why we do it. This book will attempt
to provide an introduction to some of the questions Žižek asks and the
answers he offers in reply.

WHEN ŽIŽEK SHUDDERS (WE DON'T HAVE TO): POPULAR CULTURE *AND* PHILOSOPHY?

Part of the lure of Žižek's work lies in his analyses of common culture
and everyday experiences, the way, as he admits, 'the theoretical line
of argumentation is sustained by numerous examples from cinema and
popular culture, by jokes and political anecdotes often dangerously
approaching the limits of good taste' (*TZR*: viii). Such an approach is
richly appealing in contrast to some philosophy which descants in
rather pinched and windless tones about death and the extremities of
high-minded poetry. However, what is also intriguing is the way in
which he negotiates 'the limits of good taste' and incorporates the
everyday within his work. For, as Žižek contends, the impression of
a slightly unsavoury enjoyment generated by his discussions of toilets
and Tarantino actually masks 'a "machinic" deployment of the line of
thought which follows its path with utter *indifference* towards the
pathology of so-called human considerations' (*TZR*: viii).

For example, when Žižek makes a comment about the cave in the
film *Alien*, such as 'the utero-vaginal associations aroused by this cave
are almost too intrusive' (*SOI*: 79), the word 'almost' here designates
the split evident throughout his work between the cold, dispassionate
theorist and the audience for whom he writes. If 'the utero-vaginal
associations' are 'too intrusive' precisely for whom are they 'too intrusive'? The answer, of course, is *us* – Žižek's audience. He risks
alienating us with this remark – it is too prurient, too close to an
obscenity. At the same time, however, it is not too prurient a compar-
ison for the cold theorist in Žižek, for whom every piece of cultural
detritus, no matter how appalling to the sensibilities of his audience,
is grist to the mill of theory.

The 'almost' therefore designates a split in Žižek's work – it is a kind
of shuddering point: the Žižek who acknowledges and bears the sensibilities of his readers shudders at the Žižek for whom the only thing that

matters is the theoretical point, niceties be damned. The trick with Žižek's style is that he, as it were, shudders for us, in our stead, thereby allowing us to wallow in the enjoyment of his politically incorrect observations, free from the guilt they normally induce. It is as if he says, 'Of course, I agree with you that all this talk about toilets, sado-masochism and erections is utterly obscene, nevertheless, it is incumbent upon us to theorize all aspects of life'. In so doing, Žižek makes his books enjoyable to read because he has already relieved us of the burden of self-reproach which normally clings to enjoyment in the form of guilt.

The 'almost' in the above sentence thus functions as what he terms a *fetishistic disavowal* – he knows what he is saying is 'too intrusive', nevertheless he *still* says it. There is a rhetorical figure which approximates to this disavowal called *apophasis*. Apophasis is the device of mentioning a subject by saying you will not mention it – for example, 'under no circumstances will I be drawn to discuss the minister's infidelity'. Apophasis thus articulates a kind of hole in a discourse. By saying you will not mention something, you trace the contours of what you will not mention. It, as it were, traces the limits or horizon of your speech. In theorizing popular culture and what might be called the more tawdry aspects of life, Žižek is attending to the limits of traditional philosophy – what traditional philosophy said it would *not* talk about, such as masturbation and Mel Gibson.

Žižek's subject matter, then, is the hole in the discourse of philosophy. It is that which is normally excluded from the realm of theory in order to constitute the proper topic of theory. This apparently transgressive practice, however, only works because it is undertaken from a thoroughly conservative point of view, the point of view of orthodox philosophy itself. If Žižek just analysed the detritus of culture without a rigorous philosophical viewpoint, if, in other words, his theory was as 'low' as his subject matter, the whole project would be boring – we would be indifferent to it. The initial fascination of Žižek's work proceeds precisely from the commingling of registers, from saying what should not be said by philosophy. It is analogous to the way in which, in the middle of the nineteenth century, writers, such as the French poet Baudelaire (1821–1867) began to employ synaesthesia. Synaesthesia is the description of one sense in terms associated with another sense, such as 'I hear blueness' or 'I see things loudly'. Synaesthesia only established itself as a practice against a background in which Romantic poets had rendered the depiction of individual senses insipid and mundane. The admixture of high philosophy and low culture in Žižek's work is itself a kind of synaesthesia, a blending of different types of discourse in order to render them more distinct.

What should not be missed here, however, is that, in a final twist, the perspective from which philosophy should not say that which should not be said is, in fact, the point of view of the readership of Žižek's books – those of us who have a pre-established conception of what philosophy is about. Philosophy itself is indifferent to its object. It is this indifference, this viewpoint, which is that of the cold, detached Žižek, the one for whom the 'almost' is irrelevant. The apophasis of philosophy, then, the hole in its 'official' discourse, is not one constructed by philosophy but by us. By soiling philosophy with his constant references to popular culture, Žižek is, in fact, purifying it of the 'official' prejudices of its readers, reinvigorating it with a zeal that does not shirk from anything. In this sense, the subversive character of Žižekian theory stems from it being more orthodox than orthodox theory. Žižek assumes the mandate of philosopher with a conviction that philosophy itself does not want. He takes philosophy seriously and his discussions of ephemeral culture are a sign of that enduring seriousness.

IS THIS NOT THE WAY TO READ ŽIŽEK?

One of Žižek's characteristic gestures is to formulate an interpretation by way of a negative question: are not the different toilet designs of France, Germany and England actually ways of expressing three different existential attitudes – 'German reflective thoroughness, French revolutionary hastiness, English moderate utilitarian pragmatism'? (*TPOF*: 5). When we examine the tripartite class system, are we not dealing with the Lacanian trio of the Imaginary, Symbolic and Real? Is not *The X-Files* really a demonstration of the fact that the suspended authority of the father always returns in the Real? In each case of interrogatory defiance, the answer provided by Žižek is 'Of course it is!' (an affirmation which one suspects is always secretly followed by 'and you would be a fool to think otherwise'). What these questions always designate in Žižek's work is the passage of translation. They mark the point where Žižek translates one system of meanings into another system of meanings – where, for example, Lacan's system is translated into Hegel's system or Marx's system is translated into Lacan's system or, more often than not, the Hollywood system is translated into the

Žižekian system. While, as Žižek himself is careful to note, he is not always dealing with perfect correspondences, these points of translation afford great explanatory insight. If you cannot understand things one way, Žižek seems to say, have a look at them from this angle and see if it makes sense from there.

Surprisingly, then, in spite of his lively, but essentially prosaic style of writing, Žižek is a rather poetic author. In saying this I am following the Russian linguist Roman Jakobson (1896–1982), who conceived of poetry as a predominance of metaphor over metonymy. In order to understand the difference between metaphor and metonymy we can look at the way in which sex is represented in mainstream films. If you have an instance in a movie of a couple making love, but want to suggest the act rather than show it, the metaphorical way would be to show two rain drops conjoining on the window pane, and the metonymical way would be to show abandoned clothes strewn on the floor. In other words, a metaphor designates a resemblance in qualities, whereas a metonymy identifies a part of something in place of the whole thing. Jakobson argued that whereas the novel relies on the principle of metonymy, that is the horizontal axis of language along which we combine words to make a sentence, poetry draws its power from the vertical axis of language from which we substitute one word for another in accordance with their similarity.

Žižek's work, while neither charged with individual moments of poesy nor scented with much talk of daffodils, is profoundly poetic in its structure. It substitutes one system of thought for another, one concept for the next, chiming philosophies together with all the skill of a metaphysical bell-ringer. Amid all this interchangeability, Žižek builds up a rich and dense texture of associations, one which he weaves around the 'truth' of its object, until, finally, encircling it like Native Americans surrounding the camp-fire of John Wayne in one of the films which always form part of the Žižekian tapestry. When you read a Žižek book you are, therefore, unlikely to find out what happens merely by skipping to the last page. Any narrative you find on your journey around the campfire is localized, confined to single points or chapters.

The assiduous reader of Žižek's work will thus notice that, over the broad sweep, he employs a number of concepts that turn up time and again in different guises. What this means is that for the first-time reader of Žižek there is no need to become impatient with every detail of each individual argument. Sooner or later, you will come across an 'Is this not . . .?' moment which will open up a whole series of equivalences and enable you to understand a previous discussion from a more productive angle. This, then, is the standard tactic of Žižek – his books are planned around a subject, rather than the development of an argument, they articulate the contours of a hole, circling around it, as the Argentinean philosopher Ernesto Laclau suggests when describing Žižek's first English monograph *The Sublime Object of Ideology*:

> It is certainly not a book in the classical sense; that is to say, a systematic structure in which an argument is developed according to a pre-determined plan. Nor is it a collection of essays, each of which constitutes a finished product and whose 'unity' with the rest is merely the result of its thematic discussion of a common problem. It is rather a series of theoretical interventions which shed mutual light on each other, not in terms of the *progression* of an argument, but in terms of what we could call the *reiteration* of the latter in different discursive contexts.
>
> (*SOI*: xii)

At times, this approach might seem rather frustrating. For example, he entitles a chapter of one of his books 'Why is Woman the Symptom of Man?' but he does not actually provide you with an answer in that chapter. Rather he approaches the subject indirectly, in a kind of apophasis, articulating the answer in other terms. Later on in the book, in another chapter, he provides a direct response to the question, but this time as the answer to another question – 'Why Are There Always Two Fathers?' – a question, in turn, that he only provides a direct answer to elsewhere. The reason he does this is not out of some perverse desire to thwart his readers' expectations, but rather to establish the connections between things. This is not just a matter of showing how things fit together, but of confirming the fundamental Žižekian thesis that the truth of something is elsewhere, that the identity of something is outside of itself. There is, as it were, a hole in every thing, a little piece missing that can be found beyond itself, revealing the truth of that thing.

SUBJECT OF A BIOGRAPHY: BIOGRAPHY OF A SUBJECT

We have arrived, then, at one of the fundamental theoretical knots which binds Žižek's work together: the question of identity. Žižek's own identity is interesting in this regard. He was born the only child of middle-class bureaucrats (who hoped he would become an economist) on 21 March 1949 in Ljubljana, the capital of Slovenia and, at that time, part of Yugoslavia. Yugoslavia was, then, under the rule of Marshal Tito (1892–1980), one of the more 'liberal' communist countries in the Eastern Bloc, although, as Žižek points out, the freedoms the regime granted its subjects were rather ambivalent, inducing in the population a form of pernicious self-regulation. One aspect of state control that did have a positive effect on Žižek, however, was the law which required film companies to submit to local university archives a copy of every film they wished to distribute. Žižek was, therefore, able to watch every American and European release and establish a firm grasp of the traditions of Hollywood which have served him so well since.

Žižek's interest in the films of Hollywood was matched only by a dislike for the films and, particularly, the literature of his own country. Much of Slovenian art was, for him, contaminated by either the ideology of the Communist Party or by a right-wing nationalism. Slovenian poetry specifically is still, according to Žižek, falsely venerated as 'the fundamental cornerstone of [Slovene] society' (Hanlon 2001: 4). Consequently, from his teenage years onwards, Žižek devoted himself to reading only literature written in English, particularly detective fiction. Pursuing his own cultural interests, Žižek developed an early taste for philosophy and knew by the age of 17 that he wanted to be a philosopher. Studying at the University of Ljubljana, Žižek published his first book when he was 20 and went on to earn a Bachelor of Arts (philosophy and sociology) in 1971, and then went on to complete a Master of Arts (philosophy) in 1975. The 400-page thesis for the latter degree was entitled 'The Theoretical and Practical Relevance of French Structuralism', a work which analysed the growing influence of the French thinkers Jacques Lacan, Jacques Derrida, Julia Kristeva, Claude Lévi-Strauss and Gilles Deleuze. Unfortunately, although Žižek had been promised a job at the university, his thesis was deemed by the officiating panel to be politically suspicious and he therefore lost the job to another candidate who was closer to the party line. According to his fellow Slovenian philosopher Mladen Dolar (b. 1951), the authorities were concerned that the charismatic teaching of Žižek might improperly influence students with his dissident thinking.

Bitterly disappointed by this rejection of his talents, Žižek spent the next couple of years in the professional wilderness, undertaking his National Service in the Yugoslav army, and supporting his wife and son as best he could by occasionally translating German philosophy. However, in 1977 several of his influential connections secured him a post at the Central Committee of the League of Slovene Communists where, despite his supposedly dissident politics, he occasionally wrote speeches for leading communists and, during the rest of the time, studied philosophy. In these years, Žižek became part of a significant group of Slovenian scholars working on the theories of the French psychoanalyst Jacques Lacan (1901–1981) and with whom he went on to found the Society for Theoretical Psychoanalysis in Ljubljana (for a more detailed understanding of Lacan's influence on Žižek see Chapter 1). This group, among whose best-known members are Dolar and Žižek's second wife Renata Salecl (b. 1962), established editorial control over a journal called *Problemi* (in which Žižek was not afraid to author bad reviews of his own books, or even to write reviews of books that did not exist), and began to publish a book series called *Analecta*. Žižek himself is unsure as to why so many Lacanians should have gathered in Ljubljana, but he does point out that, in contrast to the other countries in the former Yugoslavia, there was no established psychoanalytic community to hamper or mitigate their interest in the usually controversial work of the Frenchman.

Although still disbarred from a traditional university position, in 1979 Žižek's friends procured him a better job as Researcher at the University of Ljubljana's Institute for Sociology. At the time, Žižek thought that this was an intellectual cul-de-sac in which the communist regime placed those who were inconvenient to them. As it transpired, however, this job, which would be the envy of most academics, meant Žižek was able to pursue his research interests free from the pressures of teaching and bureaucracy. It was there that, in 1981, he earned his first Doctor of Arts degree in philosophy. It was also in 1981 that Žižek travelled to Paris for the first time to meet some of the thinkers he had been writing about for so long and writing to – (he has several books by Jacques Derrida, for example, dedicated to him). Although Lacan was chief among these thinkers, he died in 1981 and it was actually Lacan's son-in-law, Jacques-Alain Miller, who was to prove more decisive in Žižek's development.

Miller has been a divisive figure among Lacanians post-Lacan, for he controls Lacan's legacy and has, to some extent, assumed the mantle of the French psychoanalyst. He conducted open discussions about

Lacan in Paris, but he also conducted a more exclusive thirty-student seminar at the École de la Cause Freudienne in which he examined the works of Lacan on a page by page basis. As the only representatives of Eastern Europe, both Žižek and Dolar were invited to join this seminar and it is there that Žižek developed his understanding of the later works of Lacan which still informs his thinking today. Miller also procured a teaching fellowship for Žižek and became his analyst. It was during these analytical sessions with Miller, which often only lasted ten minutes, that Žižek learned the truth of his oft-reported assertion that educated patients report symptoms and dreams appropriate to the type of psychoanalysis they are receiving. The result of Žižek's fabrication was that the sessions with Miller often ended up as a game of intellectual cat-and-mouse.

This game ended in something of an impasse when Žižek completed his second Doctor of Arts (this time in psychoanalysis) at the Université Paris-VIII in 1985. Miller, with whom Žižek had successfully defended his thesis, was the head of a publishing house but he refused to publish Žižek's dissertation and so Žižek had to resort to a publisher outside the inner circle of Lacanians. This second major disappointment of his professional career threw Žižek back on his own resources. These resources were already being put to more obvious political ends back in Slovenia where Žižek became a regular columnist in a paper called *Mladina*. *Mladina* was a platform for the growing democratic opposition to the communist regime, a regime whose power was gradually diminishing throughout the second half of the 1980s in the face of growing political pluralism in both Yugoslavia and the Soviet Union. In 1990, the first democratic elections were held in Slovenia and Žižek stood for a place on the four-man Presidency – he came a narrow fifth. Although he stood as a Liberal Democrat candidate, this position was more strategic than a matter of conviction as he was attempting to defeat the conservative alliance between the nationalists and the ex-communists. Žižek does not, as he has often said, mind getting his political hands dirty. Nor did he mind becoming the Ambassador of Science for the republic of Slovenia in 1991.

Although Žižek continues to provide informal advice to the Slovenian government, his energies over the past decade have been firmly geared towards his research. Indeed, since 1989 and the publication of *The Sublime Object of Ideology*, Žižek has launched over 15 monographs, and a number of edited works written in English, on an eager public. He has also written books in German, French and Slovene, as well as having his work translated into Dutch, Japanese, Korean, Portuguese, Spanish, Slovak, Serbo-Croatian and Swedish. The prolific intensity of Žižek's written output has been matched by his international success as a lecturer where he has faithfully transcribed the molten energy of the word on the page to the word on the stage across four different continents. Apart from his post at what is now the Institute for Social Sciences at the University of Ljubljana, Žižek has also held positions at SUNY Buffalo; the University of Minnesota, Minneapolis; the Tulane University, New Orleans; the Cardozo Law School, New York; Columbia University, New York; Princeton University; the New School for Social Research, New York; and at the University of Michigan, Ann Arbor since 1991. He also maintains his editorial role for the *Analecta* series in Slovenia, as well as help-ing establish *Wo es war* (a series based around the combination of Lacan-ian psychoanalysis and Marxism) and *SIC* (a series devoted to Lacanian analyses of culture and politics) in German and English.

At all stages in Žižek's life, then, we can detect the insistence of a theme. When he was growing up he preferred the films of Hollywood to the dominant culture of poetry in his own country. As a student he developed an interest in, and wrote about, French philosophy rather than the official communist paradigms of thought. When he began his professional career he preferred to interpret Lacan in terms of other philosophers instead of sticking to the orthodox Lacanian line. And, as we have seen, as a philosopher himself, he constantly refers to popular culture rather than those topics customarily studied by the subject. In each case, therefore, Žižek's intellectual development has been marked by a distance or heterogeneity to the official culture within which he works. He has always been a stain or point of opacity within the ruling orthodoxy and is never fully integrated by the social or philosophical conventions against which he operates.

The point is that although Žižek's unauthorized approach has cost him the chance to become part of the established institutions on at least two occasions (once with his Master's thesis and once with his second Doctorate), he has defined his position only in his resistance to those institutions. This is not necessarily a question of Žižek initi-ating some kind of academic rebellion, nor even of proving how in the long run his talents have surpassed the obstacles erected against them, but rather of claiming that the character or identity of Žižek's philosophy is predicated upon the failure of the institutions to accommodate his thought. The eventual success of Žižekian theory proceeds partly from its early failure, from the fact that Žižek was able to perceive himself as alien to the system in which he worked.

In short, it was this alienation, this difference to the discourse of philosophy of which it was and is a part, which forged the identity of Žižek's own thought. In other words, because Žižekian theory was not part of the objective system, it was in itself subjective. The reason that this is so pertinent is that Žižek describes the formation of what is known as the 'subject' in a similar way. Indeed, one of Žižek's main contributions to critical theory is his detailed elaboration of the subject. All of which begs the question: what is a 'subject'? Žižek's answer to this query is, initially at least, fairly straightforward. If you take away all your distinctive characteristics, all your particular needs, interests and beliefs, what you are left with is a subject. The subject is the form of your consciousness, as opposed to the contents of that form which are individual and specific to you.

This might sound a rather far-fetched abstraction that you are not likely to meet strolling down the street but Žižek claims that this subject is none other than the citizen of democracy. Democracies are not composed of individual people, Žižek argues, because

> 'democracy' is fundamentally 'antihumanistic', it is not 'made to the measure of (concrete, actual) men', but to the measure of a formal, heartless abstraction. There is in the very notion of democracy no place for the fullness of concrete human content, for the genuineness of community links: democracy *is* a formal link of abstract individuals.
>
> (*LA*: 163)

By definition, then, all democratic citizens are equal to each other. A democracy takes no notice of an individual's race, gender, sexuality, religion, wealth, table manners or sleeping habits. All it is interested in is what is left when all these idiosyncratic features have been stripped away, and it is that part of the citizen which is equal to and with, and is the same as, all other citizens which Žižek designates by the term 'subject'. We might, if we remember that this is just an analogy, describe the subject as a view of the world, a place from which the world is seen.

As the description 'a place from which the world is seen' implies, a subject exists only in so far as it maintains a distance towards the world. You cannot see the world if you are part of it any more than you can see your own retina just by looking with it. A subject, for Žižek is, therefore, a piece of the world which has detached itself from the world and is a place where that world can now be seen. This is what makes a subject subjective as opposed to objective. The subject is a particular or individual view of the world. We can perhaps see here why this idea forced itself upon Žižek and why it has become one of the mainstays of his work. For Žižek himself has always maintained a distance towards the world – the world, that is, of official Slovenian culture, of the politics of academia, of Lacanian orthodoxy, and of the institution of philosophy. And it is only by maintaining that alienation from the 'systems' within or against which he operates that he has been able to forge his own identity as a thinker.

THIS BOOK

This book, then, will focus on Žižek's theories of the subject, one of his most important contributions to critical philosophy. Žižek's own books often operate with a roaming brief, covering a vast range of topics in any one chapter, so I have tried here to collate his thoughts more systematically. Beginning with a discussion of the key influences on Žižek's thought and an overview of the subject in its abstract form, each chapter will thereafter examine the subject in its postmodern, ideological, gendered and ethnic guises. These chapters are followed by an assessment of the impact of Žižek's theories and a list of Žižek's major works written in English. References to these works are indicated throughout the book by initials, while all other texts are conventionally referenced.

Hopefully, this volume will introduce and explain Žižek's theories, but it is less of a substitute for his own books, and more of a recommendation for reading them. He is often referred to in iconic terms and his readership is often depicted as a 'cult following', but I hope this book will go some way towards popularizing the wonder of Žižek. For he is altogether one of the brightest and most invigorating thinkers working today. He writes with an admirable brio, never fails to offer a fresh insight when a platitude will do, and engages fully with the world in which we live.

KEY IDEAS

1

WHO ARE ŽIŽEK'S INFLUENCES AND HOW DO THEY AFFECT HIS WORK?

ŽIŽEK'S INFLUENCES: PHILOSOPHY, POLITICS AND PSYCHOANALYSIS

Žižek's work draws on three main areas of influence – philosophy, politics and psychoanalysis. In each of these disciplines, Žižek finds the larger part of his inspiration in the writings of a single individual: Georg Hegel for philosophy, Karl Marx for politics, and Jacques Lacan for psychoanalysis. Although the ideas, methodologies and general effects of each of these thinkers overlap in Žižek's books, each can also broadly be said to have a specific influence on his thinking. Thus, Hegel's philosophy influences the type or method of thought that Žižek practises, Marx's work provides the motivation or reason behind his books, and Lacan's psychoanalysis furnishes the terminology and conceptual framework with which Žižek tackles the objects of his analysis. The aim of this chapter, then, is to outline some of the more pertinent ideas proposed by Hegel, Marx and Lacan, and to show how these ideas are employed by Žižek in his work.

HEGEL

Georg Wilhelm Friedrich Hegel (1770–1831) was a German philosopher whose work, for many commentators, represents the culmination of the tradition of Western Idealism. Idealism is a system of philosophy which seeks to examine the world in terms of ideas about it, rather than analysing the world as a thing or as a series of things. Broadly speaking, Idealist philosophers tend to argue that things, or the material world as it is more properly called, do not exist independently of the ideas the mind has about them. They believe that consciousness is the foundation for reality. One of Hegel's biggest contributions to this way of thinking was to propose that individual ideas could be joined together to form one Absolute Idea. In fact, he not only contended that this was possible, but that it was necessary too, because he thought we could only truly understand a bit of the world by understanding all of it, or what he termed the *totality*.

In order to reach a state in which it was possible to understand the totality, Hegel developed the notion of *dialectical thinking*, adapting it for use from the early Greek philosophers. The dialectic, as it was originally practised by Zeno (490–430 BC) and Socrates (470–399 BC), was no more than a method of seeking knowledge by a system of question and answer, a bit like the game 'Twenty Questions' where each question is refined by the previous answer. In Hegel's work, however, it became a method of divine interpretation, a cosmic law, and the secret motor of history all rolled into one. It is conventional to conceive of Hegel's dialectic in terms of a three-step process. You begin with a thesis, or an idea, you then counter that with an antithesis, or a qualification of that idea, and then you combine the two in a synthesis, or larger, more encompassing idea. So, for example, you might contend as your thesis that '*all* films are good'. As your antithesis you might then argue that '*Titanic* was actually a rather bad film'. Your synthesis would then be that '*most* films are good'. The synthesis would then become your new thesis and the process would start over again until you discover the whole truth of the matter – or the totality – which may well be that 'only some films are good'.

This, then, is the conventional view of Hegel's dialectic, one in which different viewpoints can always be reconciled by a greater truth. However, it is not Žižek's understanding of Hegel, nor indeed is any of what I have written so far, apart from the dates of Hegel's birth and death. For Žižek, Hegel as a thinker is far more radical than that, and so is his dialectic. For, in Žižek's reading of Hegel, the dialectic does not produce a reconciliation or a synthesized viewpoint but, instead, an acknowledgement that, as he puts it, '*contradiction* [*is*] *an internal condition of every identity'* (*SOI*: 6, emphasis added). By this he means that an idea about something is always disrupted by a discrepancy and that this discrepancy is necessary for the idea to exist in the first place. Which is to say, in a well-known phrase, that there is, and must always be, an exception which proves the rule.

So, to take our previous example, if the synthesis is that 'all films are good' and the antithesis is that '*Titanic* was actually rather a bad film', then Žižek's synthesis would be that 'all films are good because *Titanic* is actually rather a bad film'. Of course, initially this does not make sense, or, to put it another way, it is contradictory. But it is in this contradiction that the truth of the assertion lies: if there were no bad films then we would not know what a good film is because we would have nothing to compare it with. Therefore, for there to be good films there must be at least one bad film and, in this case, *Titanic* is literally the exception that proves the rule.

If you still feel nonplussed by this then I can sympathize with you. There is no doubt that Žižek's dialectic is a difficult concept to grasp the first time around. Our whole culture – everything from *yin* and *yang* to Tony Blair's 'Third Way' – is based on the notion that the truth is absolute, that if you see things one way and I see them another, then there is a middle way, a way of harmoniously reconciling our division, which can encompass both viewpoints. For Žižek, however, the truth is always to be found in contradiction rather than the smooth effacement of differences. It is what might be called an *oxymoronic* style of thought. An oxymoron is simply a phrase that employs contradictory terms, such as 'dry rain', 'cold fever', or, infamously, 'military intelligence'. Hegel's, and subsequently Žižek's, work is full of oxymorons, like 'the Spirit is a bone' and 'Wealth is the Self'. These are not just phrases, however; they are indicative of the whole approach to thinking that Žižek calls dialectical and which he employs when analysing everything from Hitchcock to European toilet designs. As such, this approach helps to account for the number of surprising statements which form the seductive headlines to Žižek's books, such as, for example, as we shall see later, that virtual reality is more real than reality itself, that the Christian tradition should be cherished by Marxism, or that the notoriously misogynist (woman-hating) work of the German philosopher Otto Weininger (1880–1903) will prove more instructive to feminism than most feminists.

MARX

Karl Marx (1818–1883) was a student of Hegel who went on to found modern communism. Broadly speaking, Marx was sharply critical of the way in which society was organized. He argued that capitalist or free-market economic production was riven by inequalities which allowed the minority to accumulate vast wealth at the cost of the oppression and wretched domination of the majority. The injustice of these divisions was, according to Marx, then disguised, promoted and ratified by the cultural, political and legal framework of society, or what he termed the *superstructure*. For Marx, the superstructure was, in large measure, determined by the very ruling classes who stood to benefit from maintaining inequality in the first place. With scant regard for detail, Marx proposed an alternative to capitalism – borrowing the term 'communism' to describe it – in which there would be no divisions or inequalities and in which each individual would be allowed to realize his or her creative potential.

By declaring himself to be 'unabashedly Marxist' (*TZR*: x), Žižek is admitting to a conviction in the truth and value of Marx's critique of capitalism and a belief in the possibility of a better, alternative method of organizing society. Indeed, while it would be fair to say that Žižek employs his interpretation of Hegel's dialectic as a tool in, for example, explaining how ideology works, Marx's critique of capitalism is the very reason why he writes at all. Which is to say that Žižek sees his work as contributing to that body of criticism which has attempted to alter the way we understand the world in order that we might wish finally to change that world for the better.

The influence of Marx can be detected in Žižek's work, then, as the motivation for a particular species of thought. Sometimes called *praxis*, this type of thought does not merely seek to categorize or reflect experience, but rather seeks to alter it. This may sound an ambitious project for a dozen books, but Žižek's battleground is the realm of ideas and culture, or the superstructure. For Marxists, the whole point of the superstructure – which includes the family, the education system, government, sport and the arts – is to secure the reproduction of the existing method of economic organization – what Marx called the *base*, which in the present instance is capitalism. If this seems a strange way to look at pop songs or the latest George Clooney film, then it is because, as Žižek would argue, you have been successfully inscribed within capitalist *ideology*, or the system of thought that glues or binds the superstructure together, making you think that it is the natural way of running society.

Ideology has many definitions in the Marxist tradition. A substantial number of these definitions centre around the proposition that ideology is simply an incorrect way of thinking about things. So, for example, while I might think that adverts are small, factual documentaries, you could reasonably point out the error in my thought here and show that they are actually a way for companies to manipulate my desires, alter my purchasing habits and persuade me to buy their products. As you can see here, such a view of ideology is not strictly a question of mistaking facts. If I think that a football is really a grenade, I am simply confused rather than ideologically misguided. What is ideological is the way we interpret facts. If I argue that football is simply a game, you might say that I am failing to interpret the way in which the game of football is inscribed within a whole series of social networks, providing a forum for nationalism, homo-erotic bonding, commercial exploitation of the working class, and so on. With this view, then, ideology is a kind of error in perception that can be corrected in a similar way to that by which you might change the lenses in your glasses if you cannot see properly.

If, in this definition of ideology, thought is either right or wrong, one of the other main definitions of ideology holds that ideology is actually a means of describing the very horizon of thought itself. In this sense it would, for example, be impossible for me to conceive of adverts as anything other than small, factual documentaries. However much you tried to reason or argue with me, however much you pulled my ears or threatened to cut the bristles off my toothbrush, it would be unthinkable for me to consider adverts in any other way. In a similar, but far less benign respect, many Marxists argue that capitalism now represents the horizon of our thought and that, as such, we are, at a practical level, unable to conceive of an alternative way of organizing society. In this sense, ideology is not something that you can think your way out of, as it represents the actual limit of thought in the same way that blindness represents the limit of sight. Given these widely differing views, it is perhaps unsurprising that it has become something of an honourable pastime in Marxist circles to propose a new theory of ideology every decade or so and then, just as routinely, to have that theory criticized, vilified and ultimately forgotten.

Clearly, this is a problem for Marxists, because it means that, without an acceptable theory of ideology they are unable to explain precisely how, in crude terms, the superstructure ensures the perpetuity of the base. This, then, is where Žižek makes his most telling contribution to the Marxist tradition. Loosely defining ideology as the way in which individuals understand their relationship to society, Žižek identified that while Marxism was able to furnish this definition with a solid grasp of the mechanics of society, it had very little to offer in the way of understanding the workings of individuals. As the instinctive and psychological processes of individuals are the very stuff on which ideology goes to work, it seemed essential to find a theory of these processes. The place where Žižek found such a theory was in the work of Jacques Lacan.

LACAN

Jacques Lacan (1901–1981) was a French psychoanalyst who controversially rewrote the ideas of the founder of psychoanalysis, Sigmund Freud (1856–1939). Part of that controversy stems from the fact that Lacan's work is a notoriously tortuous read, full of mind-bending puns, obscure allusion and slippery conceptual interplay. Indeed, it is often said, that you have to understand Lacan before you read his books. As this is just the kind of paradoxical challenge that Žižek likes, he has taken it upon himself to provide that understanding to Lacanian novices. Part of the remit for many of Žižek's books is, therefore, to explain Lacan's theories. In doing so, Žižek has done much to popularize the *particular* brand of psychoanalysis practised by Lacan. I emphasize this because psychoanalysis is usually narrowly conceived as a field of knowledge, one that comprises a method for treating neurotic patients and a set of theories about mental processes. In the hands of Lacan, however, psychoanalysis assumes cosmic ambitions, vaulting over the boundaries of its own discipline and engaging with politics, philosophy, literature, science, religion and almost every other field of learning to form a vast theory that has a hand in analysing every arena of endeavour in which human beings take part. The foundations Lacan laid for this hubristic enterprise are the three 'Orders' by which all mental functioning can be classified: the Imaginary Order, the Symbolic Order and the Order of the Real.

THE IMAGINARY, SYMBOLIC AND REAL ORDERS

It is perhaps easiest to think of these three Orders as force-fields which permeate every mental act, each one bringing to bear its own particular type of influence on an individual's well-being. Each of the three – the Imaginary, the Symbolic and the Real – can be used as nouns, naming a specific Order, as well as being used as adjectives, describing a particular thing or experience in terms of that Order. Furthermore, as the expression 'Order' suggests, not only are these Orders part of a system of classifying mental experience, they are also a means of ranking that experience in terms of a quasi-morality. Indeed, there are times in Lacan's work when the adjective 'Imaginary' can seem like a form of abuse, and the term 'Symbolic' can seem like the conferral of a blessing. Nevertheless, it is the Real that tops the pecking Order and it is almost always spoken of by Lacan in a tone of veneration and esteem.

In order to avoid confusing the Lacanian term with the everyday word, I will always write the former with a capital letter (Imaginary, Symbolic, Real), and the latter in the lower case (imaginary, symbolic, real). You should be aware, however, that Žižek does not always follow this practice himself.

THE IMAGINARY

At one level, the Imaginary designates the process by which the ego is conceived and born. This process is commonly called 'the mirror stage'. It begins when human beings are still infants of about six months old. As Lacan reminds us, human beings are born prematurely in the sense that they are unable to co-ordinate their movements until they are several years old. Infants overcome this by identifying with an image of themselves in a mirror (whether that is an actual mirror or the 'mirror' of another human being). Compared to the awkward, almost drunken sensations of dislocation they feel within their own bodies, this image offers the infant a sober picture of itself as a fully synchronized and united body. In doing so, it anticipates the child's future development and affords it a pleasing sense of coherency, or, in other words, an ego.

However, while seeming a stabilizing fiction, this process of identification actually resides within the child as a desperately capricious force, constantly undermining the very rectitude and unity it seeks to impart. This is because the discrepancy remains between the child's sensation of itself and the image of wholeness with which it identifies. As the ego is formed by this identification, an identification that assumes powers the child does not yet have, the ego is constitutionally sundered, riven by the division between itself and the image of itself. It is thus left forever trying to reconcile the other to its same.

I write 'forever' here because the ego does not change its character once we have become adults. It remains that part of you which is always questing for wholeness and unity, trying to overcome the division which created it in the first place. In its wider application, then, the Imaginary designates a restless seeking after self, a process of amalgamating more and more instances of replication and resemblance in order to bolster up the fable of its unity. As such, the Imaginary is the Order for which both Lacan and Žižek reserve an unaffected scorn. Unhappily for us, Lacan also adjudged that the modern era represents the Imaginary zenith of humankind because it is the era in which people have become obsessed with themselves and with seeing themselves and their creations take over the world.

THE SYMBOLIC

The Symbolic is perhaps the most ambitious of all the Orders because its purview includes everything from language to the law, taking in all the social structures in between. As such, the Symbolic constitutes a good part of what we usually call 'reality'. It is the impersonal framework of society, the arena in which we take our place as part of a community of fellow human beings. For example, most people are inscribed in the Symbolic before they are even born, because they are given a name, belong to a family, a socio-economic group, a gender, a race and so on. If that sounds like a positive description, Lacan indicates that we are also in some sense imprisoned by the Symbolic when he argues that what binds the Order together is the *signifying chain*, or what he terms the *law of the signifier*.

THE TWO OTHERS

Throughout his work, Žižek refers to the Lacanian distinction between the 'little other' and the 'big Other'. The 'little other', the other written with a lower case 'o' is always the Imaginary other. This designates an alterity within ourselves, or, more precisely, within our egos. The 'big Other', the Other written with an upper case 'O' refers either to the Symbolic Order as it is experienced by individual subjects, or to another subject in so far as that subject represents the Symbolic. For example, the law is an institution which is part of the Symbolic Order so it is, therefore, the Other. Equally, a policeman, because he represents the institution of the law, is also the Other. His Otherness proceeds from the fact that he is a placeholder or representative of the law. This Otherness is, therefore, more radical than the otherness pertaining to the Imaginary because it cannot be assimilated by the process of identification.

Lacan borrowed the term 'signifier' from the Swiss linguist Ferdinand de Saussure (1857–1913). Saussure argued that language was made up of signs, and that each sign was composed of two parts – the *signifier* and the *signified*. For Saussure the signifier was the mental image of the sound of the sign, and the signified was the concept associated with that sound. The two parts of the sign are held together by an arbitrary bond. In other words, there is no intrinsic reason why the sound 'cat' should signify the concept of the shabby tabby who waits by its food bowl every day expecting to be fed. In contradistinction to Saussure, Lacan valued the signifier more highly than the signified.

Saussure also insisted that language was a *relational* or *differential* system. By this he meant that no sign can be defined in isolation from other signs. So, for example, we know that a cat is a cat because it is *not* a dog or a rabbit. Just as we know that something is bad if it is *not* good. Equally a man is a man because he is *not* a woman, and left is left because it is *not* right. (It should be noted that although Žižek accepts this position, he does so with the proviso that we understand the relations between the two terms to be predicated upon absence and presence. In this way, the second term of a pair merely fills out the absence of the first term and vice versa. For example, 'night' fills out the void where 'day' is not present.)

This '*not* something' or differential aspect of language is crucial for Lacan because, if words only refer us to other words rather than to the world, we are cut off from that world and left marooned on the shores of language. Indeed, in this sense, language is an independent system, forming its own closed world. Which is to say that, instead of reflecting experience, words constitute it. If this sounds a little far-fetched, then think about the difference it makes describing a person either as a terrorist or as a freedom fighter. Even though that person stays the same, our attitude towards them is completely different depending on how we refer to them. You may well counter that at least that person is still a 'person'. However, that is just another choice because that 'person' could also be a 'hominid', a 'mammal' or even an 'animal'. In this way, language carves up the world making it impossible to assume a neutral position towards it.

The list of words by which a person can be referred to here – 'hominid', 'mammal', 'animal', and 'person' itself – forms an example of what Lacan refers to as the *signifying chain*. If you recall, the signifying chain is what binds the Symbolic Order together and, simply put, it refers to the total network of available signifiers. In one sense this is a list of substitutions or possible words that can be used to refer to the same thing. So for example, 'heat' can be substituted by the words 'warmth', 'fervour', 'incandescence' or 'fever'. Each of these words has links to other words. For instance, 'fever' can be substituted by 'illness' or 'disease' and even 'cold', which, of course, is the exact opposite of 'heat'. Eventually, the whole network of signifiers can be traced back along the various chains so that when you use one word you are implicitly using every other one as well.

The implications of this for an understanding of the Symbolic Order are twofold and contrary. First, it means that if the Symbolic Order is bound together by the signifying chain, or if, in other words, we cannot approach anything except by way of the unstable and arbitrary law of the signifier, then we are doomed never to know 'the world as it really is' but rather perpetually condemned to the prison-house of language. Second, on the other hand, if the relationship between signifier and signified is arbitrary and unstable, then the character or type of Symbolic Order in which we live is neither permanent nor necessary. Over recent years, for example, the role of women in society has fundamentally changed from a lesser status than men to an equal one. In this case, the signifier 'woman' no longer refers to the signified 'second-class or inferior human being', but rather to just 'female human being'.

THE REAL

The Order of the Real describes those areas of life which cannot be known. In one sense, of course, that means everything, for, as we have just discovered, all our knowledge of the world is mediated by language. We never know anything directly. In this sense, the Real is the world before it is carved up by language. There is something of this experience in the following description of Mommy's understanding of the mountain from the novel *Choke* by the American author Chuck Palahniuk (b. 1962):

> For one flash, the Mommy had seen the mountain without thinking of logging and ski resorts and avalanches, managed wildlife, plate tectonic geology, microclimates, rain shadow, or *yin-yang* locations. She'd seen the mountain without the framework of language. Without the cage of associations. She'd seen it without looking through the lens of everything she knew was true about mountains. What she'd seen in that flash wasn't even a 'mountain'. It wasn't a natural resource. It had no name.
>
> (Palahniuk 2001: 149)

Here, the Mommy has access to a mountain in its immediacy, before the mountain becomes enmeshed in language and culture. Apart from the fact that she identifies the mountain in its singularity, in its difference from everything else around it, this approximates well to an encounter with the Real. If you can imagine a state in which it is impossible to differentiate between, for example, a tree, the ground in which it has its roots, the squirrel in the leaves and the sky that surrounds it, then that is the Real. As you can see, it is not something I can describe because, by default, I have to use words to do so, identifying each separate element of the world. It is for this reason that Lacan argues that the Real resists Symbolization.

Why, then, should we pay any attention to the Real? After all, if we are condemned to living in the Symbolic what difference does it make what happens in the Real? The trick here is to remember that the Symbolic and the Real are intimately bound up with each other. The Symbolic works upon the Real; it introduces a cut into it, as Lacan claims, carving it up in a myriad different ways. Indeed, one of the ways in which you can recognize the Real is by noting when something is indifferent to Symbolization. So, for example, returning to human beings, you can see that some part of them is Real by counting up the different ways in which we are Symbolized – as 'hominids', 'apes', 'mammals', 'animals' and so on. We enter into the Symbolic Order when we are named or otherwise classified in this way, but previous to that we are in the Real.

Similarly, anything that is interpreted differently discloses the presence of the Real. AIDS is a good example of this. Some people interpret it as a punishment for homosexuals, a divine retribution for carrying on a non-Christian way of life. Others see it as part of a plot by the CIA to stem population growth in Africa, while other people consider it the result of humankind's interference in Nature. All these explanations circle around the same brute fact of the disease which carries on regardless of the reasons attributed to it. In other words, AIDS is an irruption of the Real. It is meaningless in itself and all these interpretations of it are attempts to Symbolize it, attempts, we might say, to divine a message in the Real where none exists. For the Real is meaningless and senseless – it just persists, and meaning can only be found within the reality of the Symbolic Order.

TRAUMA

A traumatic event represents, for Žižek, the archetypal relationship between the Symbolic and Real Orders. It defines the point where the Real disrupts the smooth running of the Symbolic. There are several theories of trauma, but the one Žižek is concerned with is Freud's concept of *Nachträglichkeit* or, as it is usually translated, 'deferred action'. The most famous example of this can be found in Freud's case history of the so-called 'Wolf-Man'. Freud argued that the Wolf-Man's neurosis (his fear of being eaten by wolves) was caused by an event (witnessing, at age one and a half, his parents having sex) which initially meant nothing to him but later (at age four), in a deferred action, became traumatic. In other words, as Žižek argues here, the traumatic character of the event was not intrinsic to the initial event or *primal scene*:

> In the case of the Wolf Man ... the cause, of course, was the traumatic scene of the parental *coitus a tergo* – this scene was the non-Symbolizable kernel around which all later successive Symbolizations whirled. This cause, however, not only exerted its efficiency after a certain time lag; it

literally *became* trauma – that is, cause – through delay: when the Wolf Man, at age two, witnessed the *coitus a tergo*, nothing traumatic marked this scene; the scene acquired traumatic features only in retrospect, with the later development of the child's infantile sexual theories, when it became impossible to integrate the scene within the newly emerged horizon of narrativization-historicization-symbolization.

(*TMOE*: 31)

Which is to say that, when the Wolf-Man originally witnessed his parents copulating it made little sense to him. It was part of the Real, resisting Symbolization. Three years later, however, he had developed a series of simple sexual theories, mostly concerned with castration, which enabled him to interpret what he had seen his parents doing. It was at this point – the point of Symbolization – that the scene became traumatic and he developed his phobia of wolves. What is important to recognize here is that the Real or the event remains the same; it is the Symbolic which changes the meaning of the event. Which is why, twenty years later, Freud was able to help the Wolf-Man reintegrate the event into the Symbolic in a non-neurotic fashion. For even though the event in itself did not alter, the way it was understood, given meaning or Symbolized did. This, then, is how the relationship between the Real and the Symbolic always proceeds: the Real just persists, but how we interpret the Real changes with the Symbolic.

We can also look at the Real from the opposite direction. For while, on the one hand, the Real is what precedes the Symbolic, it is the fullness of things that the Symbolic goes to work on, slicing it up into articulate pieces, on the other hand, it is also the remainder, or what is left over once the Symbolic has completed this process. The Real in this sense comes after the Symbolic, it is the excess that remains behind and resists Symbolization, appearing only as a failure or void in the Symbolic. If the Real comes both before and after the Symbolic Order, is this not a contradiction in terms? The answer is 'Yes!' and for those who have been faithfully following this chapter so far, it will remind them of Hegel's dialectic. This is because, for Žižek, the Real is the arena of the dialectic, where opposing terms can coincide. In distinction to this, the Imaginary is where two terms can be reconciled in a harmonious synthesis, and the Symbolic is where two terms are defined differentially, where one *is* something because it is *not* something else. Given Žižek's preference for oxymorons, it is perhaps easy to see why he therefore favours the Real over the other two Orders, because it is the only Order where contradictions are not effaced.

There is one final point I would like to make here about the relationship between the Real and the Symbolic which is that if the Symbolic was not an incomplete or insufficient account of the Real, if, that is, we could apprehend the Real directly, then we, as subjects, would disappear. The reason for this is that if everything was exactly as it was meant to be, if everything could be grasped in its fullness, if there was no discrepancy between the way you saw the world and the way I saw it, if, in other words, every signifier perfectly matched every signified, and every sign matched every referent, there would be no signifying chain. All there would be is the Symbolic Order in perfect correspondence with the Real. The thing that make us human, or more precisely, the thing that makes us subjects, is the signifying chain and the decisions we take in regard to it and that would have disappeared and, therefore, us along with it. So, if we all agreed that the AIDS crisis is a CIA plot, that all human beings are a bunch of apes, that sprouts are the finest produce of the vegetable kingdom, and so on, we would no longer be human beings or subjects at all, we would just be automatons or robots, blindly obeying the dictates of the Symbolic Order. This is not to say that we would physically de-materialize, but as thinking beings who take decisions and make choices, we would have evaporated.

There is, perhaps, something of this experience to be had in the sensation produced when you have been driving a car for an hour or so and you suddenly realize that you cannot remember the journey at all. This is because, in Lacanian terms, you were an automaton, automatically and unthinkingly obeying the laws of driving which, in this case, stands in as an instance of the Symbolic Order. During the drive you became merely part of the Symbolic and you, as a subject, disappeared. However, had a truck coming in the opposite direction accidentally veered off onto your side of the road, this could be considered an intrusion of the Real. You would have had to decide what to do, perhaps by braking or swerving and, in that moment of decision, in choosing how to deal with this intrusion of the Real, you would have reappeared as a subject. In this sense, then, Žižek argues that the subject exists at the interface, or on the borders between the Symbolic and the Real. Quite simply, if there was no interaction between the two Orders, the subject would not exist at all.

THE PHILOSOPHER OF THE REAL

Žižek is sometimes referred to as the 'philosopher of the Real'. This reference is partly a play on the word 'real', in so far as Žižek discusses 'real' topics, such as European toilet designs or Arnold Schwarzenegger films, rather than just abstract ideas with no immediate bearing on the way we live our lives. However, it also refers, as is now probably clear, to the Lacanian Real, a concept which he has expanded and made his own. What should be borne in mind here is that in writing about the Real, Žižek is almost always writing about it in relation to the Symbolic. This is partly what makes Žižek's work unique, because, until he made his timely entrance on the international critical scene, most theorists tended to concentrate on the relationship between the Symbolic and Imaginary. As we shall see in the following chapters, by switching the focus of attention to the antagonism between the Real and the Symbolic, Žižek was then able to formulate an extremely coherent account of the subject in all its gendered, ideological, ethnic and postmodern guises.

SUMMARY

The three main influences on Žižek's work are Hegel, Marx and Lacan.

* Hegel provides Žižek with the type of thought or methodology that he uses. This type of thinking is called dialectical. In Žižek's reading of Hegel, the dialectic is never finally resolved.
* Marx is the inspiration behind Žižek's work, for what Žižek is trying to do is to contribute to the Marxist tradition of thought, specifically that of a critique of ideology.
* Lacan furnishes Žižek with a framework and terminology for his analyses. Of particular importance to Žižek are the concepts of the Symbolic and Real. Žižek locates the subject at the interface of these two Orders.

2

WHAT IS A SUBJECT AND WHY IS IT SO IMPORTANT?

THE *COGITO*

The Introduction of Žižek's *The Ticklish Subject* begins with his assertion that 'a spectre is haunting Western academia . . ., the spectre of the Cartesian subject' (*TTS*: 1). The Cartesian subject, or *cogito* as it is also known, is, he proclaims, constantly liable to attempts to exorcize it from contemporary thought by New Age obscurantists, postmodern deconstructionists, Habermasians, Heideggerians, cognitive scientists, Deep Ecologists, post-Marxists and feminists. In short, just about every-body reviles the *cogito*. Aficionados of Žižek's contrary mode of thought will, therefore, not be surprised to learn that, in opposition to all these theoretical factions, he fully endorses the model of the Cartesian subject. All of which raises the question: what is the *cogito* and why does everyone (except Žižek) seem to want done with it?

Although the idea for it was originally proposed by Saint Augustine (354–430), one of the founders of the Christian Church, the *cogito* in the form that we know it was first advanced by René Descartes (1596–1650), the French philosopher, mathematician and soldier who is often referred to as the Father of Modern Philosophy. Descartes' starting point for the *cogito* was a cold winter's day. It was so icy that he climbed into a very large stove to keep himself warm and stayed there all day. During his confinement Descartes commenced upon the philosophic procedure which is named after him: Cartesian doubt. The point of this procedure was to establish what could really be known.

Descartes began by isolating the evidence of his senses: was he really sitting by a fire in his dressing gown? He concluded that he could not be sure. He had often dreamt of just such a scenario and, in his dream, this had seemed real to him. However, even if the dream itself were an illusion, what of the concepts employed by the dream, the mathematical concepts such as shape, number and size which apparently match those of reality? Descartes concedes that although these may seem to be correct, there is a possibility that they are all the invention of an evil genius designed to fool him. If this were the case though, Descartes argues that he could not be deceived if he did not exist in some form. Given that his body may be an illusion, Descartes concludes that at the very least his thought must exist, if it is to be deceived:

> While I decided thus to think that everything was false, it followed necessarily that I who thought thus must be something; and observing that this truth: *I think, therefore I am*, was so certain and so evident that all the most extravagant suppositions of the sceptics were not capable of shaking it, I judged that I could accept it without scruple as the first principle of the philosophy I was seeking.
>
> (Descartes 1968: 53–54)

This phrase and first principle – '*I think, therefore I am*' or '*cogito, ergo sum*' – is what the term '*cogito*' designates.

THE *COGITO* AND THE POST-STRUCTURALISTS

There are many ways of interpreting the *cogito*, but we are interested here only in two – the post-structuralist version and Žižek's version. For the post-structuralists, the *cogito* is the basis of the centred subject, or, as it is more commonly known, the 'individual', and it is regarded by them as the spoilt brat of philosophy. The individual, as the name suggests, is indivisible. In our day-to-day lives, we tend to think of ourselves as individuals because we feel we are complete, in charge of ourselves and not subject to the whims of outside forces. When Descartes states 'I who thought thus must be something', we understand that 'I', the 'I' of the *cogito*, to be an individual. It is the 'I' that does the thinking – the thoughts belong to him rather than him to the thoughts. In other words, the 'I' of the *cogito* is the master of itself. An individual is therefore self-transparent – nothing impedes its understanding of itself because it is in total control and has total autonomy over its actions. There are no dark banana skins of the soul waiting to slip up the psyche, there are no words which threaten to betray the meaning of their speaker, and there are no gusts of history which might suddenly blow the individual from its perch. The world of the individual is an immaculate, windless, danger-free environment.

It is, therefore, a state of perfection. Its main advantage is that nothing impinges upon the autonomy of the individual. Every person, as the saying goes, is an island – self-sufficient, independent and free to do what it wills. Its main disadvantage, however, is that nothing impinges upon the autonomy of the individual. Every person is an island – self-sufficient, independent and free to do what it wills. In other words, the very features of the individual which seem to confer upon it such blessings are also those which blight it. This is because the individual conceived in this way is utterly subjective; everything remains within its dominion and subject to its control. There is no objectivity at all.

If this seems merely to be a philosophical problem, the consequences for this model of subjectivity are equally compelling within 'reality' as well. For example, until recently, it was generally accepted (by men at least) that only men were masters of themselves. Women, on the other hand, were supposed to be subject to passions and feelings which they could not properly control. That is to say, women were not centred subjects but decentred subjects. They were, therefore, not 'proper' individuals and were treated accordingly as second-class citizens, subject to the rule of the masterful men. In fact, the mastery of women formed part of the larger project to dominate the natural world itself (of which women were held to be a part). The results of this project, which is sometimes referred to as the Enlightenment Project, can be witnessed in the devastation wreaked upon the environment. If it seems a little harsh to rebuke a philosophical model with the destruction of the planet, it is perhaps worth remembering that only a subjectivity which thinks it answers exclusively to itself would risk the destruction of nature and not expect to be held accountable for it. For, in destroying nature, we are effectively sawing away at the branch on which we sit.

Against the background of this rampant subjectivism, then, it is perhaps not surprising that philosophers (among them the post-structuralists) discerned the need for a corrective dose of objectivism. They built upon developments in other sciences which had long been chipping away at the monumental authority of the centred subject. For instance, the Polish astronomer Nicolas Copernicus (1473–1543) pushed humanity to the margins of the solar system by showing that the Earth orbited the Sun rather than the other way round. Similarly, Charles Darwin, the English naturalist (1809–1882), proved that humans are a species of ape subject to the laws of nature and not a breed apart from other animals. And, in creating the field of psychoanalysis at the beginning of the twentieth century, Freud's disclosure of the unconscious demonstrated that much of our psychic life is inaccessible and beyond our control. All of these developments, along with others, helped to breach the seemingly impervious subjectivism of the individual, showing it to be subject to forces outside of itself, or else that it belonged to a world of which it was not the centre.

Building upon these theories, the post-structuralists rejected the notion of the *cogito* with its associated individualism and advanced in its stead the idea of the decentred subject. As I have already suggested, this subject is not an autonomous being with the power of self-determination but rather an effect of the structure of discourse where competing discourses intersect and speak through the subject. In this way, the meaning of the subject is not inside or at the centre of itself; instead the meaning of the subject is decentred or located outside of the subject in the competing discourses, in, for example, the discourse of the unconscious or ideology. The subject is therefore determined or impelled by these discourses. It cannot determine itself but is subject to (or in a 'subject position' to) the dominant ideologies and histories of the day. In its bleakest form, therefore, the decentred subject is little more than a puppet of overwhelming forces with, as Žižek points out, its only individual outlet being the way in which it experiences life at the end of the strings:

> In 'post-structuralism', the subject is usually reduced to so-called subjectiva-tion, he is conceived as an effect of a fundamentally non-subjective process: the subject is always caught in, traversed by the pre-subjective process (of 'writing', of 'desire' and so on), and the emphasis is on the individuals' different modes of 'experiencing', 'living' their positions as 'subjects', 'actors', 'agents' of the historical process.
>
> (*SOI*: 174)

In other words, the post-structuralist subject is, as Derrida argues, merely 'a "function" of language' (Derrida 1973: 145), a kind of Symbolic automaton doomed to ventriloquize the discourse of the big Other.

One of the problems with this model, of course, is that the objective world encroaches so far upon the subjective world of the individual that there is little or no subjectivity left. If everything is objective, if there is no subjective element to my character at all, I cease to have any particularity or any individuality: I am nothing but the point where the system, or the Symbolic, speaks. But this cannot be right either. How, for example, can I decide to drink coffee in the morning rather than tea if I am a decentred subject that is merely a puppet pulled by the strings of ideology, language, the unconscious and so on? Where is the 'I' that makes this decision or indeed any decision? Clearly, in a world of pure objectivity this 'I' does not exist, but equally clearly we do not live in such a world either because we do make such decisions.

Both of the models of subjectivity we have looked at so far, then, are hamstrung by forms of extremism, tending either to over-value the subjective or prize too highly the objective. A fully rounded subjectivity must maintain a productive harmony between the two, preserving the realm of the personal in order that we may exist at all and securing it upon the ground of the impersonal so that we may have somewhere to exist in. To find such a subject we must return to Žižek's reading of the *cogito* and examine how he understands it completely differently from the post-structuralists.

MADNESS: THE VANISHING MEDIATOR BETWEEN NATURE AND CULTURE

Žižek's reading of the *cogito* is rather more indebted to the method by which Descartes arrives at his famous pronouncement than just the *cogito* itself. Specifically, for Žižek, the method of Cartesian doubt affords us a telling insight into how we transform from beings immersed in nature (or objectivity) to beings supported by culture (or subjectivity). The works of philosophers, such as the Germans Immanuel Kant (1724–1804) and Hegel, are, according to Žižek, haunted by the question of this transformation. How is it that at one moment we are just part of nature, part of an objective world, and in the next moment we are speaking beings able to adopt a subjective attitude towards the rest of the world? Where does this distance come from? Unable to postulate that culture is magically conferred upon human beings, Hegel and Kant are forced to invent a creature that is not quite of nature but not yet of culture (or *logos* – the Word, as Žižek variously phrases it) either. In Hegel's work, for example, the place of this in-between being is occupied by what Hegel terms 'negroes', a people half in thrall to nature and half attempting to enthral it.

For Žižek, however, the missing link between nature and culture is to be found in the process of Cartesian doubt. Žižek describes the process of Cartesian doubt as a withdrawal into self – a withdrawal symbolized by Descartes's own physical withdrawal into the oven. Descartes cuts himself off from the world, systematically severing all links with his environs until all he is left with is the *cogito*. It is here, in the gesture of total withdrawal, that Žižek locates the hidden passage from nature to culture. This gesture is, for Žižek, one of madness – the specific madness of Hegel's 'night of the world':

> This night, the inner of nature, that exists here – pure self – in phantasmagorical representations, is night all around it, in which here shoots a bloody head – there another white ghastly apparition, suddenly here before it, and just so disappears. One catches sight of this night when one looks human beings in the eye – into a night that becomes awful.

(quoted in *CATU*: 258)

It is only when reality is eclipsed by this 'night of the world', when the world itself is experienced only as loss, as absolute negativity, that it becomes possible, and indeed necessary (if we are to escape from madness), to construct a symbolic universe or a universe of culture. Descartes's withdrawal-into-self is precisely such an experience of radical loss. For Žižek, Descartes's *cogito* is not the substantial 'I' of the individual, but an empty point of negativity. This empty point of negativity is not 'nothing' but the opposite of everything, or the negation of all determinacy. And it is exactly here, in this empty space devoid of all content, that Žižek locates the subject. The subject is, in other words, a void.

It is this void that, for Žižek, enables the transition from a state of nature to a state of culture. This is because if there was no gap between a thing (or an object) and the representation of that thing (or word), then they would be identical and there would be no room for subjectivity. Words can only exist if we first 'murder' the thing, if we create a gap between them and the things they represent. This gap, the gap between nature and the beings immersed in it, is the subject. The subject, in other words, is the missing link, or 'vanishing mediator' as Žižek calls it, between the state of nature and the state of culture. Žižek's point here is that the transition from nature to culture is not a story that can be told in terms of an evolutionary narrative, such as that offered by Hegel. Rather, the withdrawal-into-self which culminates in the *cogito* has to be presupposed as the vanishing mediator between the two, the missing link around which the transition is organized. In other words, we have to 'get rid' of the Real before we can construct a substitute for it in the form of the Symbolic Order. Žižek reads this vanishing mediator as a passage through madness and, by so doing, he conceives the subject (which is the vanishing mediator) as mad. Madness, therefore, is for Žižek a prerequisite for sanity, that is, for the 'normalcy' of a civilized subject.

THE VANISHING MEDIATOR

The concept of the 'vanishing mediator' is one that Žižek has consistently employed since *For They Know Not What They Do*. Žižek borrows the concept from an essay – 'The Vanishing Mediator; or, Max Weber as Storyteller' – by the North American Marxist critic Fredric Jameson (1934–). In the essay,

Jameson analyses the critique of Marxism advanced by Max Weber (1864–1920), the influential German sociologist. Briefly, this critique consists in the claim that Protestantism was the condition of possibility for the emergence of capitalism. As Protestantism is a religion and capitalism is a mode of production, this explanation inverts the traditional Marxist hierarchy in which the base gives rise to the superstructure. Jameson's response to this is to show how capitalism developed out of Protestantism in a dialectical movement which is fully consistent with Marxism. He argues that this dialectic is driven by what he terms a vanishing mediator – the missing link between two terms. In this case, he proposes that Protestantism is the vanishing mediator between feudalism and capitalism. Before the advent of Protestantism, religion was a separate sphere from that of economics. Protestantism, however, universalized religion, bringing the world of work within its purview, prompting people to live ascetically by accumulating wealth and working hard. In so doing, it created the conditions of possibility for capitalism. Ironically, of course, the advent of capitalism led to the obsolescence of Protestantism in particular, and religion generally, as Jameson notes:

> It [Protestantism] is thus in the strictest sense of the word a catalytic agent that permits an exchange between two otherwise mutually exclusive terms; and we may say that . . . the whole institution of religion itself . . . serves in its turn as a kind of overall bracket or framework within which change takes place and which can be dismantled and removed when its usefulness is over.
>
> (Jameson 1988b: 31)

A vanishing mediator, then, is a concept which mediates the transition between two opposed concepts and thereafter disappears.

Žižek draws attention to the fact that a vanishing mediator is produced by an asymmetry of content and form. As with Marx's analysis of revolution, form lags behind content, in the sense that content changes within the parameters of an existing form, until the logic of that content works its way out to the latter and throws off its husk, revealing a new form in its stead. Commenting on Jameson's essay, for example, Žižek proposes that:

> The passage from feudalism to Protestantism is not of the same nature as the passage from Protestantism to bourgeois everyday life with its

privatized religion. The first passage concerns 'content' (under the guise of preserving the religious form or even its strengthening, the crucial shift – the assertion of the ascetic-acquisitive stance in economic activity as the domain of the manifestation of Grace – takes place), whereas the second passage is a purely formal act, a change of form (as soon as Protestantism is realized as the ascetic-acquisitive stance, it can fall off as form).

(*FTKN*: 185)

Žižek sees in this process evidence of Hegel's 'negation of the negation', the third moment of the dialectic. The first negation is the mutation of the content within and in the name of the old form. The second negation is the obsolescence of the form itself. In this way, something becomes the opposite of itself, paradoxically, by seeming to strengthen itself. In the case of Protestantism, the universalization of religious attitudes ultimately led to it being sidelined as a matter of private contemplation. Which is to say that, Protestantism, as a negation of feudalism, was itself negated by capitalism.

THE BIRTH OF GOD: READING THE *COGITO* VIA SCHELLING

Žižek's point of reference for this theory of the genealogy of the subject is the work of the German philosopher Friedrich Wilhelm Joseph von Schelling (1775–1854). For Žižek, Schelling functions as a kind of vanishing mediator in the history of philosophy. His work is the invisible connection between idealism and materialism, maintaining the *form* of the idealism of previous philosophers while introducing the *content* of a materialism that is later taken up by Marx, the German philosopher Friedrich Nietzsche (1844–1900) and Freud. It is because Žižek reads Schelling as a vanishing mediator that he does not disregard what might otherwise appear to be the arcane religious mythology of his work. As Žižek comments, 'every attempt to discard the part or aspect considered "not true" inevitably entails the loss of the truth itself' (*TIR*: 7).

With this in mind, it is perhaps less surprising that Žižek expends most of his labour on analysing the second draft (of three) of Schelling's *Die Weltalter* (or *Ages of the World*), the text in which Schelling considers nothing less than the genesis of God. The origin of God, as Žižek reminds us, is well known from the Gospel according to St John: 'In the beginning was the Word'. Žižek designates this beginning with an upper case 'B' – it is the 'Beginning'. However, for Žižek, Schelling's philosophy is all about the fact that the Beginning is not at the beginning. Before the Beginning 'is the chaotic-psychotic universe of blind drives, their rotary motion, their undifferentiated pulsating' (*TIR*: 13). These drives are the ultimate Ground (*Grund*) of reality – the basis for everything. Nothing precedes them, except this 'nothing' itself, this abyss (or *Ungrund*).

The nature of this abyss, as the title of Žižek's book on the topic suggests, is one of unmitigated freedom. It is not a freedom that 'belongs' to anyone, it is not the predicate of a subject; it is, rather, 'a pure impersonal Willing (*Wollen*) that wills nothing' (*TAOF*: 15), the brute contingent fact which, for Schelling, must be presupposed to exist. In the beginning (which, remember, is prior to the Beginning) God is part of this Freedom – He is not yet the individual Being. He is a pure Nothingness enjoying the state of non-being. Such contentment, however, contains the seeds of an inherent discontent. This is because the blissful peace of pure freedom is based on the fact that it is an unassertive Will which wants nothing. Nevertheless, wanting 'nothing' is an assertion in itself, as Žižek explains:

> The pure potentiality of the primordial Freedom – this blissful tranquillity, this pure enjoyment, of an unassertive, neutral *Will which wants nothing* – actualizes itself in the guise of a *Will which actively, effectively, wants this 'nothing'* – that is, the annihilation of every positive, determinate content.
>
> (*TIR*: 23)

Wanting nothing and wanting 'nothing' are two sides of the same coin, contractions and expansions which constitute the rotary motion of drives which precede the Beginning. The Will that wants something is the positive, expansive Will, while the Will that wants precisely nothing is the negative, contracting Will. The result is a recursive deadlock.

Žižek interprets this recursive deadlock, this rotary motion, as failed attempts to Begin, as so many false starts. It is a vicious circle in which God fails to differentiate between Himself and His Predicate. God, in other words, is merely part of the *Grund*, of the basis of reality, but not yet an independent Entity in His own right. For God to achieve His independence He has to disentangle Himself from the *Grund*. As Žižek explains:

> In order to posit itself as an actual free Entity disengaged from blind necessity – in short as a person – the Absolute has to get things straightened out, to clear up the confusion in itself, by way of acquiring a distance towards what in it is not God Himself but merely the Ground of His existence – that is by ejecting the Ground from Himself.
>
> (*TIR*: 36)

It is here that we find the analogy with Descartes's own attempt to secure the first principle of philosophy – the solid ground of existence. For the only way that God can establish the Ground for His existence is, like Descartes, by destroying all determinate content, by withdrawing from the world, as it were, 'by ejecting the Ground from Himself'. Žižek characterizes this act as a form of divine insanity, one that can be identified as analogous to the madness of Hegel's 'night of the world'. In other words, as Žižek deftly phrases it: 'God himself was "out of his mind"' (*TAOF*: 11). He has to risk madness before He can exist. It is this lunacy which, for Žižek, constitutes the vanishing mediator between Nothingness and God Himself.

What is crucial to recognize here – for it is a motif that runs throughout Žižek's oeuvre – is that the subject (in this case God) is constituted by a loss, by the removal of itself from itself, by the expulsion of the very Ground or essence from which it is made. The subject, in this sense, is always a nostalgic subject, forever trying to recover its loss. However, this Ground must remain outside of the subject for the subject to retain its consistency as a subject. The subject, in other words, must externalize itself in order to be a subject at all. What this means is that the subject is no longer opposed to the object, as it is in the other two models of subjectivity we have looked at; rather, subject and object are implicated in each other – the subject is the object outside of itself. The subject maintains what Žižek, following Lacan, calls a relation of *extimacy* towards itself. 'Extimacy' is a mixture of the two words 'external' and 'intimacy'. This external intimacy or extimacy designates the way in which the core of the subject's being is outside itself. If this sounds a little difficult to conceptualize, it is perhaps easiest to think of it in analogy to your eyeball. You can see everything except the part of you that does the seeing – your own eyeball. The only way you can see your eyeball is by looking in a mirror where it is outside of yourself. The subject is in an analogous position to this: it is a perspective on reality which cannot be grasped in itself but only in the 'mirror' of reality.

FROM SUBJECT TO SUBJECTIVIZATION

The place where the subject is externalized is the Word, the Word that announces the Beginning:

> How, precisely, does the Word discharge the tension of the rotary motion, how does it mediate the antagonism between the contractive and the expansive force? The Word is a *contraction in the guise of its very opposite, of an expansion* – that is to say, in pronouncing a word, the subject contracts his being outside himself; he 'coagulates' the core of his being in an external sign. In the (verbal) sign, I – as it were – *find myself outside myself*, I posit my unity outside myself, in a signifier which represents me.
>
> (*TIR*: 43)

The problem with this is that if I find myself outside of myself, I am no longer self-identical. The signifier which represents me is just that, a representation, but it is not actually me. However, if I am to be a subject at all, I cannot avoid this irretrievable loss, for it is only on account of this loss that I actually become *something* rather than remain as *nothing*.

We can, perhaps, make more sense of Žižek's reading of Schelling by rendering it in Lacanian terms. In fact, at one point, Žižek observes that the passage from the closed rotary motion of the drives to the pronunciation of the Word is simply the passage from the Real to the Symbolic. The Real – or the *Grund* – is the world before it is carved up by language, and language – or the Word – is the medium of the Symbolic Order. One might also add that the rotary motion of the drives can be characterized as an Imaginary experience of the Real. The endless pulsating of the drives, their interminable contraction and expansion, is akin to the civil war that the ego visits upon itself in the mirror stage as it oscillates between identity and difference. God, at this stage, like the infant at the mirror, is a purely self-relating entity. He has no objective mooring for His Being – everything is just subjective, or 'inside' Him, as Žižek avers:

> This God is not yet the Creator, since in creation the being (the contracted reality) of an Otherness is posited that possesses a minimal self-consistency and exists *outside* its Creator – this, however, is what God in the fury of his egotism is not prone to tolerate.
>
> (*TAOF*: 17)

It is only with the pronunciation of the Word (or a Symbolic experience of the Real), which introduces a cut into the Real and stands in for it, that God can establish His distance from it. In substantially the same way, although we, as bodies, are still part of the Real, we, as Symbolic subjects, are also differentiated from it. Which is to say that, although we are grounded in nature and can only survive within our bodies, simultaneously we are not merely our bodies; rather we *have* our bodies and can relate freely to them and it is language that enables us to do this.

READING SCHELLING VIA LACAN

Once you have grasped the basic Lacanian concepts of the Imaginary, the Symbolic and the Real, you will notice that in his philosophical writings, such as in his discussion of Schelling, Žižek always interprets the work of other philosophers in terms of those concepts. This is because, as he admits on several occasions, 'the core of my entire work is the endeavour to use Lacan as a privileged intellectual tool to reactualize German Idealism' (*TZR*: ix). This raises three related questions: what is German Idealism, why does it need reactualizing, and what does 'reactualizing' mean? The term 'German Idealism' designates the work of philosophers such as Kant, Johann Gottlieb Fichte (1762–1814), Schelling and Hegel. The reason that Žižek believes German Idealism needs reactualizing is that he thinks we are taught to understand it in one way, whereas he regards the truth of it to be something else. The term 'reactualizing' (which is borrowed from Schelling) refers to the fact that there are different possible ways to interpret German Idealism, and that Žižek wishes to realize or make 'actual' one of those possibilities in distinction to the way it is currently realized or 'actualized'.

At its most basic, we tend to be taught that the German Idealists thought that the truth of something could be found in itself. For Žižek, on the other hand, the fundamental insight of German Idealism is that the truth of something is always outside itself. So, for example, the truth of our experience lies outside ourselves, in the Symbolic and the Real, rather than being buried deep within us. We cannot look into our selves and find out who we truly are, we cannot gaze into our own navels, because who we truly are is always elsewhere. Our navels, as it were, are somewhere else in the

Symbolic formations which always precede us and in the Real which we have to disavow if we are to enter the Symbolic in the first place.

The reason that Lacan occupies a privileged position for Žižek is that the key to his work can be found in the proposition that self-identity is impossible. The identity of something, its singularity or 'oneness', is always split. To put this in another way, there is always too much of something, an indivisible remainder, or a bit left over which means that it cannot be self-identical. For example, the meaning of a word can never be found in the word itself, but rather in other words. The meaning of 'cat' cannot be discovered in the word 'cat' but in the words 'small, domestic feline'. Therefore, the meaning of 'cat' is not self-identical. This principle of the impossibility of self-identity is what informs Žižek's reading of all the German Idealists, including Schelling. For instance, as we have seen, the Beginning is not actually the beginning at all – the truth of the Beginning lies elsewhere; it is split or not identical to itself.

The process of subjecting ourselves to language and to the rest of the Symbolic Order is what Žižek calls subjectivization. Although this sounds like the formation of the post-structuralist subject, the difference is that, for Žižek, subjectivization needs to be conceived as a two-way process. On the one hand, the Symbolic Order, or the big Other, precedes us and speaks through us. For example, we might be born into a family and bear that family's name, occupy a specific socioeconomic position, follow a particular religion, and so on. On the other hand, because the Symbolic Order is incomplete or constituted by a lack (a lack which is the subject) the way in which we integrate these elements of the Symbolic and narrate them to ourselves is ours. For example, we might disown our family and change our name, invent a new religion, and so on. Even if we are some kind of cyborgs, the gap in the Symbolic means that we are not reducible to mere functions of the Symbolic or automatons, as Žižek notes when commenting upon the ambiguous status of the replicants in the film *Blade Runner*:

Despite the fact that their most intimate memories are not 'true' but only implanted, replicants subjectivize themselves by way of combining these memories into an individual myth, a narrative which allows them to construct their place in the symbolic universe.

(*TWTN*: 41)

It is the replicants' ability to create an individual story out of implanted memories that makes them seem human because that is exactly what we do too. We maintain our ability to integrate the elements of the Symbolic in an individual way and it is what Žižek terms the 'Self' that does this, what he defines as the 'centre of narrative gravity' (*CATU*: 261). In other words, the Self is what fills in the void of the subject, and while the subject never changes, the Self is open to constant revision.

SUMMARY

Unlike almost all other kinds of contemporary philosophers, Žižek argues that Descartes' *cogito* is the basis of the subject. However, whereas most philosophers read the *cogito* as a substantial, transparent and fully self-conscious 'I' which is in complete command of its destiny, Žižek proposes that the *cogito* is an empty space, what is left when the rest of the world is expelled from itself. The Symbolic Order is what substitutes for the loss of the immediacy of the world and it is where the void of the subject is filled in by the process of subjectivization. The process of subjectivization is where the subject is given an identity and also where that identity is altered or changed by the Self.

3

WHAT IS SO TERRIBLE ABOUT POSTMODERNITY?

THE POSTMODERN RISK SOCIETY

The topic of the postmodern has been a fertile area of debate among critical thinkers for the past twenty years or so. Much of that debate has centred upon the precise definition of 'postmodern'. As a general rule, most thinkers use the term 'postmodernity' to refer to the historical and social epoch in which we now live, and 'postmodernism' to designate the cultural response to that epoch. The term 'postmodernist' is usually used purely as the adjectival form of 'postmodernism', while 'postmodern' is sometimes employed just to describe aspects of 'postmodernity' and sometimes to describe aspects of 'postmodernism' too. If the interchangeability of these terms can often lead to confusion, in all cases what is clear is that by employing the term 'postmodern' (in whatever form) the writer concerned is indicating that he or she thinks there has been a substantial mutation or change in either the socio-economic basis of our lives and/or in the cultural response to that new basis.

Žižek is one of those thinkers who argue that we are living in the postmodern era. The starting point for his analysis of postmodernity is the theory of the 'risk society' advanced by the German sociologist Ulrich Beck (1944–) and the English sociologist Anthony Giddens (1938–). The risks referred to in the title of this theory are 'low probability – high consequence' risks, such as the increase in carbon emissions which might lead to global warming, the modification of plant genes with animal genes which might lead to chemically resistant insects, the pollution of food sources by artificial oestrogens which might result in the sterilization of the male population, and so on. The probability of any one of these situations coming to fruition unchecked is small, but if any one of them does the consequences would be apocalyptic for humankind.

POSTMODERNISM AND POSTMODERNITY

The two most influential theories of postmodernity are proposed by Fredric Jameson and the French philosopher Jean-François Lyotard (1927–1998). Jameson contends that the past thirty years or so have witnessed the arrival of a new wave of capitalism which he calls 'late capitalism'. The distinction of late capitalism is the scale of its reach, its hitherto unsurpassed infiltration of every area of life. For Jameson (and, indeed, for Žižek, who loosely draws upon this model), postmodernism is the cultural logic of late capitalism, or the response of culture to its colonization by the commodity. Some of the main features of postmodernism identified by Jameson are the integration of previously separate cultural genres (the mixing of high and low art, as well as the combination of distinct styles, such as Westerns and science-fiction films), the loss of a sense of history (manifest in a desire for nostalgia), and a euphoric attachment to surfaces or depthlessness (such as can be found in the predominance of the image over the word).

Although, like Jameson, Lyotard was originally a Marxist philosopher, his contribution to the theory of postmodernity is largely based on an eschewal of his Marxist past. In particular, Lyotard advances the claim that the postmodern is defined by the erosion of 'grand narratives'. Grand narratives are stories or interpretations that lay claim to explaining the totality of life or everything. One of the most famous grand narratives is Marxism, and Lyotard rejects it (along with the other grand narratives) because he claims it is totalitarian or oppressive in the sense that it requires the specificity of people and things to be ignored in favour of a generality. In response to Lyotard and the many other critics who have since taken up this notion, Žižek has written a book rebuffing this argument – *Did Somebody Say Totalitarianism?* – accusing such critics of succumbing to the cultural logic of late capitalism.

A vital aspect of each of these risks is that they are 'manufactured risks', which is to say that they are the products of human intervention in the natural world. Furthermore, they are such substantial interventions that we can no longer allow nature to correct itself and so solve the problem for us because each risk involves the derailment of nature itself. The only way to lessen the effect of these risks, therefore, is by further scientific and technological intervention, which, in turn, will produce other unforeseen outcomes. We are thus caught in a self-reflexive loop where the effective diminishment of one risk results in the generation of a fresh risk, with each new attempt to control our environment creating new uncertainties.

It is this reflexivity which is key to an understanding of postmodernity for Žižek. We are, as it were, caught in our own web. Scientists and government agencies are unable to establish with complete certainty the extent of the peril engendered by these manufactured risks, not because they are necessarily too complex, but because they are too opaque:

> The new opaqueness and impenetrability (the radical uncertainty as to the ultimate consequences of our actions) is not due to the fact that we are puppets in the hands of some transcendent global Power (Fate, Historical Necessity, the Market); on the contrary, it is due to the fact that 'nobody is in charge', that *there is no such power*, no 'Other of the Other' pulling the strings – opaqueness is grounded in the very fact that today's society is thoroughly 'reflexive', that there is no Nature or Tradition providing a firm foundation on which one can rely.

(*TTS*: 336)

In other words, we are now living in a totally subjective world where we answer only to ourselves and live without a substantial basis in either the natural world or our own customs and conventions.

THE DISINTEGRATION OF THE BIG OTHER

For Žižek, one key aspect of the universalization of reflexivity is the resulting disintegration of the big Other, the communal network of social institutions, customs and laws. Žižek compares this disintegration with Lacan's comments on God – it is not just that God is dead today, rather He always was dead, but He just did not know it. Similarly, the big Other always was dead, in the sense that it never existed in the first place as a material thing. All it ever was (and is) is a purely symbolic or fictional order. What Žižek means by this is that we all engage in a minimum of idealization, disavowing the brute fact of the Real in favour of another Symbolic world behind it. He expresses this disavowal in terms of an 'as if'. In order to coexist with our neighbours we act *as if* they do not smell bad or look ridiculous. When we stand before a judge we act *as if* he is not an ignorant old man but rather a conduit through which the law speaks. If we wish to remain loyal subjects we act *as if* the emperor really is wearing new clothes and not parading through the streets naked.

The big Other is thus a kind of collective fib or lie to which we all individually subscribe. We all know very well that the emperor is naked in front of us (in the Real) but we nonetheless agree to the deception that he is in fact wearing new clothes (in the Symbolic). What Žižek means, then, when he avers that 'the big Other no longer exists' is that in the new postmodern era of reflexivity we no longer believe that the emperor is wearing clothes. We believe the testimony of our eyes (his nakedness in the Real) rather than the words of the big Other (his Symbolic new clothes). Instead of treating this as an admirable case of puncturing hypocrisy, Žižek argues that we get 'more than we bargained for – that the very community of which we were a member has disintegrated' (*FTKN*: 12). There is, in other words, a demise in what Žižek terms 'Symbolic efficiency'.

Symbolic efficiency refers to the way in which for a fact to become true it is not enough for us just to know it, we need to know that the fact is also known by the big Other too. Žižek explains this point by reference to a joke about a madman who thought he was a grain of corn. After being cured and sent home, he returns to his doctor exclaiming that he has just met a chicken who he thought might eat him. Exasperated, the doctor exclaims that he is a human being and not a grain of corn, to which the man replies: 'Yes, *I* know that, but does the hen?' In other words, the man is still a grain of corn until his status as a human being is verified by the big Other. Similarly, I am not the fastest athlete in the world until it is verified by the established athletics institutions. Nor am I a poet until my poems have been published. Equally, I will still be a learner-driver until I have passed a driving test. In each case, even though I will be exactly the same person with exactly the same skills, the fact of my being the fastest athlete in the world, a poet or a driver does not become operative *for me or anyone else concerned* until it is registered by the big Other of the Symbolic institution.

What is crucial to understand here is that, for Žižek, it is the big Other which confers an identity upon the many decentred personalities of the contemporary subject. In other words, the different aspects of my personality do not claim an equal status in the Symbolic – it is only the Self or Selves registered by the big Other which display Symbolic efficiency, which are fully recognized by everyone else and determine my socio-economic position. The level at which this takes place is *not*, as Žižek points out,

> that of 'reality' as opposed to the play of my imagination – Lacan's point is not that, behind the multiplicity of phantasmic identities, there is a hard core of some 'real Self'; we are dealing with a symbolic fiction, but a fiction which, for contingent reasons that have nothing to do with its inherent structure, possesses performative power – is socially operative, structures the socio-symbolic reality in which I participate. The status of the same person, inclusive of his/her very 'real' features, can appear in an entirely different light the moment the modality of his/her relationship to the big Other changes.
>
> (*TTS*: 330)

A fairly common example of the way in which the status of someone can change the moment the modality of their relationship to the big Other alters are those people who enter hospitals and practise as doctors even though they are not qualified. It is not unknown for years to pass by without them being detected. In that time they perform the functions of doctors as well as anyone who is qualified for the position. The moment they are found to be unqualified, however, their whole status changes. All the mistakes they made are now seen not as the acceptable accidents of a professional, but as the inevitable casualties of a charlatan. Which is another way of saying that before these people are found to be impostors, their acts display Symbolic efficiency, but after their credentials are found to be fraudulent, the very same acts no longer demonstrate Symbolic efficiency.

THE POSTMODERN SUPEREGO: ENJOY!

Žižek does not necessarily consider that the function of psychoanalysis is to lament the demise of Symbolic efficiency; rather he thinks that psychoanalysis can offer us important insights into the effects of this demise. So what are these effects? Perhaps the most obvious effect is that, with the demise of the authority of the big Other we are no longer subject to nature or tradition but rather subjects of choice. We refer to custom only in order to snub it and we make reference to the natural world only to highlight its imperfections. We are thus cut loose from all conventional ties and, as such, everything we do becomes a matter of choice. However fundamental or trivial – from what sex our children are, whether we should have blue eyes or green, if we should have bran flakes with or without banana chips for breakfast, through to whether we should spend eternity interned in a grave, floating through space as dust or embalmed as a mummy – all are subject to our decisions.

If it sounds like a good thing to be freed from the cruelty of a capricious nature or the discriminations of conventions which only favour the few, then Žižek would be in agreement. However, Žižek is not suggesting that we have broken with just certain traditions or customs but with any collective mode of conduct at all. We are all desperately free to do whatever we choose. Apart from the general dangers of assuming a fully autonomous model of subjectivity (which were highlighted in Chapter 2), Žižek also argues that the increasing reflexivization of our lives and the concomitant demise in Symbolic efficiency also presents us with a whole new set of problems to deal with.

One of these problems is an increasing attachment to subjection. If we are no longer subject to the Law of the big Other then, according to Žižek we are likely to counterbalance this loss of official authority by invoking 'private laws' or relationships of dominance and subjection. Žižek cites the growth in sado-masochistic sexual dependencies as evidence for this. In these relationships, people derive libidinal satisfaction from freely becoming slaves or submissives to masters or dominants. In other words, this reverses what we might think of as the conventional situation in which public regulation is secretly subverted by acts of liberating transgression. For what the increase in sado-masochism indexes is the fact that we now have a public equality which is secretly subverted by acts of severe private regulation. When everyone has free choice, denying yourself that free choice becomes transgressive.

Such a paradoxical tactic is, for Žižek, indicative of the type of reflexivity with which psychoanalysis has to deal. For example, it is a commonplace in Lacan's work that it is impossible to satisfy desire because desire itself designates a state of non-satisfaction. Desire in this sense can only be terminated; it can never be satisfied. For hysterics, however, this very unrealizable character of desire is reflexively converted into a desire for desire to keep itself unrealized. Similarly, obsessional neurotics invert the regulation of desire into a desire for regulation. In all these cases, what is at stake, according to Žižek, is the reflexivity at the heart of the subject – one which he claims is ignored by the risk society theorists. So while these theorists are busy championing the reflexive freedom of the postmodern subject (or the subject of 'second modernity', as they call it), they neglect to take account of the ways in which the subject mediates that freedom through a reflexivity that was always-already there.

We can see this at work, for example, in our so-called permissive society. Constantly bombarded with images of, and invitations to indulge in, sexual enjoyment, it can no longer be claimed that sexual pleasure is in any way prohibited. On the contrary, for Žižek, sensual gratification has been elevated to the status of an official ideology. We are compelled to enjoy sex. This compunction – the injunction 'Enjoy!' – marks the return of the superego. The superego is often thought of as an internal agency of prohibition – the little voice of the law inside our heads. For Žižek, however, following the late Lacan, the superego works in a different way from the law – (that is, Symbolic authority per se rather than just the law in a particular country) – in fact, it is the obverse of the law, feeding on what the law represses. So, whereas the law is a renunciation of enjoyment which manifests itself by telling you what you cannot do, the superego orders you to enjoy what you can do. In other words, the superego 'marks a point at which *permitted* enjoyment, freedom-to-enjoy, is reversed into *obligation* to enjoy' (*FTKN*: 237).

THE LAW

Žižek refers to the law throughout his work. The term 'the law' signifies the principles upon which society is based, designating a mode of collective conduct based upon a set of prohibitions. However, for Žižek, the rule of law conceals an inherent unruliness which is precisely the violence by which it established itself as law in the first place:

> 'At the beginning' of the law, there is a certain 'outlaw', a certain Real of violence which coincides with the act itself of the establishment of the reign of law ... The illegitimate violence by which law sustains itself must be concealed at any price, because this concealment is the positive condition of the functioning of the law.
>
> (*FTKN*: 204)

> In other words, the authority of the law stems not from some concept of justice, but because it is the law. Which is to say that the origin of the law can be found in the tautology – 'the law is the law'. If the law is to function properly, however, we must experience it as just. It is only when the law breaks down, when it becomes a law unto itself, and it reaches the limits of itself, do we glimpse those limits and acknowledge its contingency by reference to the phrase 'the law is the law'.

As Žižek points out, when enjoyment becomes compulsory it is no longer much fun. To illustrate this idea, he draws on the depiction of sexual education in the film *Monty Python's the Meaning of Life*. Instead of the conventional image of an embarrassed teacher talking about birds and bees to giggling students, here the teacher confronts the pupils with an intimate and direct anatomy of sexual intercourse, even down to offering a practical demonstration. For their part, the pupils are either embarrassed or bored and end up looking out of the window as they would be expected to do in any normal, dull lesson. For Žižek, what this episode evinces is the truth 'about the "normal" state of things: enjoyment is not an immediate spontaneous state, but is sustained by a superego imperative' (*TPOF*: 173). All *Monty Python* do is lay bare what is normally hidden as unconscious.

This example also shows how the injunction of the superego to 'Enjoy!' is stultifying in its effect, leaving the addressees of the injunction either indifferent or unable to enjoy what they are told to enjoy. As evidence for this, Žižek cites the trend for opinion polls to show that people find less and less interest in sexual activity. This trend is also manifest in the popularity of Viagra where, for Žižek, the superego takes on a chemical form. Viagra restores the erectile function of the penis in impotent men, allowing them to bypass any psychological problems they have (which are probably caused by the superego imperative in the first place) and enabling them to have an erection whenever they want. As far as Žižek is concerned, this means that there is no longer any excuse for them not to have sex and that therefore 'you should enjoy sex; if you don't it's your fault!' (*TFA*: 134).

Žižek's point here, then, is that the superego's imperative to 'Enjoy!' is far more effective as a way of hindering access to enjoyment than a direct prohibition from the Law not to enjoy. The postmodern subject is thus like the daughter in the comedy programme *Absolutely Fabulous*. Her mother is not only extremely liberal, but actively enjoins the daughter to miss school, take drugs, have sex, get drunk, waste money and so on. This apparently radical behaviour, however, terrorizes the daughter, leaving her unable to enjoy any of these conventionally transgressive acts. Consequently, and to the consternation of her mother, she adopts a thoroughly conservative attitude towards life and 'transgresses' by studying diligently, remaining chaste and sober and by trying to impose a censorious regime upon her mother. In other words, the daughter assumes a masochistic position because the only route to pleasure left for her under the superego injunctions of her mother is via the intervention of a degree of pain.

KEEPING IT REAL: THE RETURN OF THE OTHER

The paradox of postmodernity is that the freedom afforded by the demise of the big Other is actually experienced as a burden which manifests itself in a desire for discipline. In this sense it is analogous to Žižek's analysis of Hegel's discussion of habit. For Hegel, habit is a kind of mechanized response to the world which frees us from the time-consuming attention to details, thereby allowing us to engage with more profound matters. As Žižek avers:

> Our intellectual creativity can be 'set free' only within the confines of some imposed notional framework in which, precisely, we are able to 'move freely' – the lack of this imposed framework is necessarily experienced as an unbearable burden, since it compels us to focus constantly on how to respond to every particular empirical situation in which we find ourselves.
>
> (*TIR*: 25)

The supreme example which Žižek provides of such a framework is language itself. You can only think freely within a language once you have mastered its rules of syntax and grammar, once you no longer have to consult a dictionary for the exact meaning of a word, and so on. Without the habit or framework of these rules, you experience the language as a burden.

The freedom of postmodernity is analogous to the freedom of speaking a language without a grammatical framework. We have no rules to follow or interpret. It is little wonder therefore that the demise of the big Other has seen the rise in numerous little others or partial big Others in order to offset that demise. Žižek proposes as evidence for this the way in which ethical dilemmas forced on us by technological gains are increasingly referred to specialist committees for their solution. What the proliferation of these committees index is the absence of accepted Symbolic prohibitions. In the light of this absence, basic rules of conduct regarding cyberspace, biogenetics, medicine and the like have to be invented by ethical boards. They answer the questions, for example, of how much genetic manipulation is acceptable in an unborn foetus, whether or not someone on a life-support machine is actually alive, or what constitutes sexual harassment on the internet. By transferring responsibility for the resolution of ethical deadlocks such as these to committees, individual subjects relieve themselves of the burden of the freedom of resolving these problems on their own.

If the construction of little big Others is one reaction to the demise of the big Other, another response identified by Žižek is the positing of a big Other that actually exists in the Real. The name Lacanian psychoanalysis gives to an Other in the Real is 'the Other of the Other'. A belief in an Other of the Other, that is in someone or something who is *really* pulling the strings of society and organizing everything, is one of the signs of paranoia. Following Jameson's influential analysis of postmodernity, it is now a commonplace to argue that the dominant pathology of today is paranoia. No film or paperback thriller, for example, is these days complete without reference to some secret organization, usually a military–industrial complex, which covertly controls governments, newspapers, markets and other significant institutions. Žižek proposes that the cause of this paranoia can be located in a reaction to the demise of the big Other:

> When faced with such a paranoid construction, we must not forget Freud's warning and mistake it for the 'illness' itself: the paranoid construction is, on

the contrary, an attempt to heal ourselves, to pull ourselves out of the real 'illness', the 'end of the world', the breakdown of the symbolic universe, by means of this substitute formation.

(*LA*: 19)

Paradoxically, then, Žižek argues that the typical postmodern subject is one who displays an outright cynicism towards official institutions, yet at the same time firmly believes in the existence of conspiracies and an unseen Other pulling the strings. This apparently contradictory coupling of cynicism and belief is strictly correlative to the demise of the big Other. Its disappearance causes you to construct an Other of the Other in order to escape the unbearable freedom its loss encumbers you with. Conversely, there is, in effect, no need to take the big Other seriously if you believe in an Other of the Other. You therefore display cynicism and belief in equal and sincere measures.

POSTMODERNISM: AN OVER-PROXIMITY TO THE REAL

One of the ways in which Žižek's understanding of the postmodern can be characterized is as an over-proximity to the Real. In postmodern art (or postmodernism) Žižek identifies various manifestations of this, such as the technique of 'filling in the gaps'. What Žižek means by this can be seen in his comparative analysis of the book and film versions of *The Talented Mr Ripley*. In Patricia Highsmith's novel, Ripley's homosexuality is only indirectly proposed, but in Anthony Minghella's film of the novel, Ripley is explicitly gay. In other words, the repressed content of the novel, the absence around which it centres, is filled in. For Žižek, what we lose by covering over the void in this way is precisely the void of subjectivity:

> By way of 'filling in the gaps' and 'telling it all', what we retreat from is the void as such, which, of course, is ultimately none other than the void of subjectivity (the Lacanian 'barred subject'). What Minghella accomplishes is the move from the void of subjectivity to the inner wealth of personality.

(*TFRT*: 148)

In other words, in Highsmith's book the status of Ripley's sexuality is, at most, equivocal. As such, the book remains 'innocent' in the eyes of the big Other because it does not openly transgress one of its norms. While we can interpret the clues in the book as indicating Ripley's homosexuality, we do not have to do so. The film, on the other hand, 'shows it all'. Ripley is here *objectively* homosexual. So whereas in the book the reader can decide *subjectively* whether or not Ripley is gay, the film allows no such room for manoeuvre and the viewer is forced to accept Minghella's reading of the text.

One of the more interesting examples of an Other in the Real is the increasing interest – evidenced in best-sellers on the subject – in the 'true' life of Christ. This interest centres upon such alleged features of the 'real' Christ as his marriage to Mary Magdalene, the exact way he was crucified, or his actual tomb – features supposedly hidden by the official Church. What such narratives attempt to do, according to Žižek, is replace the fading Symbolic efficiency of the Holy Spirit, that is the spiritual community of believers (who believe in the retroactive Grace afforded by the Resurrection), with the bodily Real of Christ and/or his descendants. The true message of this Christ is thus not his Resurrection, which for advocates of the Real Christ never actually happened, but rather the soul's journey of self-development for which the real Christ provides an example.

One of the ways in which postmodern subjects increasingly express their individuality (on the soul's journey of self-development) is through what Žižek terms the 'cut in the body', by which he means tattooing, piercing and bodily mutilation. For Žižek such cuts also signal a movement from the Symbolic to the Real. He explains this by identifying a four-part history of cuts in the body. Within pagan cultures, cuts in, or marks on, the body signified membership of that culture, indicating that you were included within its socio-symbolic embrace. Following this, Judaean society introduced the single cut of circumcision which, although functioning in the same way, was exceptional and marked a prohibition on the multitude of cuts found in pagan cultures. With the advent of Christianity, however, even this exceptional cut was internalized. In each of these cases, the cut in the body indicates a movement from the Real (the bodily flesh) into the Symbolic (membership of society). The postmodern return to the multitude of pagan cuts in the body, on the other hand, signifies a movement from the Symbolic to the Real. Instead of these cuts bearing the mark of society, they represent what Žižek terms 'a defiance of the flesh' (*TTS*: 372), the means by which an individual displays that individuality and defies his/her submission to the big Other.

THE ACT

In summary, then, the demise in Symbolic efficiency leaves the post-modern subject in a state of narcissistic self-conferral, desperately seeking an Other of the Other in the Real. It is a condition that, for Žižek, has long since been formulated by Lacan: 'when Symbolic efficiency is suspended, the Imaginary falls into the Real' (*TTS*: 374). James Redfield's best-selling book *The Celestine Prophecy* provides a concise example of this predicament. This book, which declares itself as an adventure about 'spiritual truths', finds that all contingent encounters (that is, encounters in the Real) are secretly subject to the law of synchronicity (and not to Symbolic efficiency) and, in fact, always carry a message addressed to us. In tandem with this, the book calls for us to discover in ourselves what, up until now, we have vainly been seeking to find in the Other. Žižek understands this in Lacanian terms to mean that the Other is reduced to the other, an Imaginary counterpart who is not a subject in his/her own right but, in effect, an aspect of a self-sufficient ego (the other) with a message for him/her. According to Žižek, such spiritual wisdom amounts to no more than the ideology of a commercialized society that equally finds in the Other/other messages for the self-sufficient consumer.

So how do we resolve this dilemma? For Žižek, the only way out is by means of an act. An act is a kind of re-birth of the subject. It involves a total rejection of the existing Symbolic Order and therefore of the Symbolic mandate or role assumed by the subject. The subject quite literally disappears, as Žižek avers:

> The act differs from an active intervention (action) in that it radically transforms its bearer (agent): the act is not simply something I 'accomplish' – after an act, I'm literally 'not the same as before'. In this sense, we could say that the subject 'undergoes' the act ('passes through' it) rather than 'accomplishes'

it: in it, the subject is annihilated and subsequently reborn (or not), i.e., the
act involves a kind of temporary eclipse, *aphanisis*, of the subject.

(*EYS*: 44)

The annihilation of the subject in the act is strictly correlative to Hegel's
'night of the world' (discussed in Chapter 2). Just as the 'night of the
world' is the founding gesture of subjectivity, so the act is a return to
that gesture, a repeat of the founding moment of the subject. As such,
it is an act of madness in which one withdraws from the world, risking
not only any possible return but more fundamentally what one will
return to.

In a way, therefore, the act is a way of striking at yourself, a form
of Symbolic suicide. For example, in the film *The Usual Suspects*, the
key scene which establishes the myth of Keyser Soze is when he returns
home to find his family held hostage by a rival gang. Instead of capit-
ulating, Soze makes the mad gesture of shooting what is dearest to
him, i.e., his family, thereby enabling him to massacre the rival gang
and all they hold dearest to them. In other words, as Žižek argues,
'this act, far from amounting to a case of impotent aggressivity turned
against oneself, rather changes the co-ordinates of the situation in which
the subject finds himself' (*TFA*: 150). Similarly, in Toni Morrison's
novel *Beloved*, Sethe kills her own children in order to save them from
slavery. The only way she can protect the dignity of her children within
the existing Symbolic (of slavery) is by rejecting the mandate of that
Symbolic and murdering what is most dear to her.

Perhaps the supreme example of an act – and why Žižek has recently
expended so much critical labour on the subject – is the founding
gesture of Christianity – the Crucifixion. God sacrifices what is dearest
to Him in order to found a new beginning in which a new subject –
the Holy Spirit – can flourish. The good news of Christianity, and for
Žižek its most radical point, is that we can all be born again. Unlike
New Age or Gnostic wisdom which enjoins us to rediscover or realize
the potential of our true selves, Christianity asserts that we can create
or invent new selves.

It is this aspect of the act, the negation which opens up the possibility of reinvention, which is most appealing to Žižek. It offers what
he considers to be a model of political engagement sorely lacking in
the postmodern. For Žižek, postmodern political discourse takes place
within the horizon of liberal-capitalism. We may argue about different

parts of it – such as how the health service should be funded or what level of taxation there should be – but capitalism itself is never seriously questioned. Indeed, capitalism is the framework in which these discussions make sense; it is, to recall an earlier analogy, the grammar of contemporary politics. What Žižek proposes is that if we wish to resolve the predicaments of the postmodern subject, we can only do so by rejecting the conditions of possibility of postmodernity as such, that is by changing the horizon or Symbolic in which these predicaments make sense. In other words, we have to take a passage through a political act. Such a political act is, for Žižek, nothing other than a revolution. By the very nature of an act, of course, Žižek cannot say what the world would look like after a revolution (a fact which has caused some critics to accuse him of a certain vagueness of thought). All Žižek can say at present is that he wishes to reject that which we have – capitalism – in the hope that it opens up the space for something better – a space in which subjects are not paranoid narcissists who have become beleaguered by their own enjoyment and find pleasure only in servility.

SUMMARY

For Žižek, present society – or postmodernity – is based upon the demise in the authority of the big Other. Critiquing the theorists of the contemporary risk society, who advocate the personal freedoms of choice – or reflexivity – which have replaced this authority, Žižek argues that these theorists ignore the reflexivity at the heart of the subject. Lacking the prohibitions of the big Other, Žižek argues that, in these conditions, the subject's inherent reflexivity manifests itself in attachments to forms of subjection, paranoia and narcissism. In order to ameliorate these pathologies, Žižek proposes the need for a political act or revolution – one which will alter the conditions of possibility of postmodernity (which he identifies as capitalism) and so give birth to a new type of Symbolic Order in which a new type of subject can exist.

4

HOW CAN WE DISTINGUISH REALITY FROM IDEOLOGY?

FALSE CONSCIOUSNESS AND CYNICISM

It is perhaps difficult to remember now, but it was only twenty years ago that most people were agreed that humankind's exploitation of nature was a more or less uncontested fact of our existence. The way in which that exploitation was organized, however, whether it should be communism, liberal capitalism or even fascism, was a matter of the fiercest debate. Now, as Žižek points out, the situation is practically reversed. Since the end of the Cold War (the great ideological struggle between communist and capitalist countries which reached its zenith during the years 1945–1991), few care to conceive of alternative forms of production to capitalism, although most people are gravely preoccupied with the potentially apocalyptic exploitation of nature itself. The result of this change is, as Žižek argues, that 'it seems easier to imagine "the end of the world" than a far more modest change in the mode of production, as if liberal capitalism is the "real" that will somehow survive even under conditions of a global ecological catastrophe' (*TZR*: 55). For Žižek, the prevalence of this paradox (the fact that it is easier to imagine the end of the world than a change to it) attests to the work of ideology. All of which raises the question: what exactly is ideology?

The most basic definition of ideology for Žižek is provided by Marx – 'they do not know it, but they are doing it' (*SOI*: 28). What is at stake here is a kind of innocence or ignorance of the 'reality' we live in. On the one hand there is reality and, on the other hand, there is our understanding of that reality which is in some way distorted. Ideology is precisely that distortion, that skewing of our understanding. Ideology, in this sense, is an epistemological problem – a problem of knowledge. For example, we do not know that when we troop off to college every day we are being conditioned to reproduce the capitalist system (as workers, managers and entrepreneurs), so that is why we are happy to continue doing it. We do not know that every time we vote we are endorsing the status quo, so we continue voting in the vain belief that our vote matters. We do not know that our religious beliefs are actually ways to keep us pliable citizens, so we continue to go to church every Sunday.

PINNING DOWN IDEOLOGY WITH *POINTS DE CAPITONS*

One of the questions that Žižek asks about ideology is: what keeps an ideo-logical field of meaning consistent? Given, as we saw in Chapter 1, that sig-nifiers are unstable and liable to slippages of meaning, how does an ideology maintain its consistency? The answer to this problem, according to Žižek, is that any given ideological field is 'quilted' by what, following Lacan, he terms a *point de capiton* (literally an 'upholstery button'). In the same way that an upholstery button pins down stuffing inside a quilt and stops it from moving about or bunching up in one corner, Žižek argues that a *point de capiton* is a signifier which stops meaning from sliding about inside the ideological quilt. A *point de capiton*, in other words, unifies an ide-ological field and provides it with an identity. For example, 'freedom' in itself is an open-ended word, the meaning of which can slide about depending on the context of its use. A right-wing interpretation of the word might use it to designate the freedom to speculate on the market, whereas a left-wing interpretation of it might use it to designate freedom from the inequalities of the market. The word 'freedom' therefore does not mean the same thing in all possible worlds; what pins its meaning down is the *point de capiton* of 'right-wing' or 'left-wing'. What is at issue in a conflict of ideologies is precisely the *point de capiton* – which signifier (for example, 'communism', 'fascism', 'capitalism', and so on) will win the right to quilt the ideological field (for example, 'freedom', 'democracy', 'human rights' and so on).

With such a model of ideology – what is, after Marx (although it was his German collaborator Friedrich Engels (1820–1895) who coined the term), generally referred to as 'false consciousness' – the process of ideological critique is fairly straightforward. All that is required to enlighten the bewildered subjects is to show them how their under-standing of reality is distorted. At this point, as soon as ideology is recognized as ideology, that is, as a distorted version of the truth, it dis-appears. However, as Žižek points out, today we already know that we are receiving a distorted version of reality. We already know that when we go to college we are being groomed to keep the system going. We know that when we go to a polling station our vote will not substantially alter the political system. We know that going to church helps keep us as pliable citizens. In other words, we are all, as Žižek avers, following the German theorist Peter Sloterdijk (b. 1947), cynical subjects.

As cynical subjects, we know full well that our understanding of reality is distorted, but we nevertheless stick to that falsehood and do not reject it. Instead of Marx's formula for ideology, then – 'they do not know it, but they are doing it', Sloterdijk proposes a cynical variation of it – 'they know very well what they are doing, but still, they are doing it' (*SOI*: 29). Žižek argues that we must distinguish between cynicism and what Sloterdijk terms 'kynicism'. Kynicism is a form of sarcastic or ironic response to authority, one which ridicules the hypocrisy of ruling institutions. It exposes the piety of politicians' statements, for example, to be the subterfuge for personal greed and self-promotion. In other words, kynicism designates precisely most people's attitudes towards politicians and other state institutions.

What Sloterdijk and Žižek contend, however, is that such kynicism is already taken into account by the official culture. Cynicism is the way it takes kynicism into account, for the cynical subject already accepts that the official version of reality is flawed or distorted, but still it does not dispense with that skewed vision. How, therefore, asks Žižek, is an ideological critique supposed to proceed? If we cannot demonstrate to subjects in ideology that they are being misled, *because they already know it*, does this mean that we are living in a post-ideological world, one where the distinction between ideology and reality no longer matters? The answer, according to Žižek, is 'No'.

In order to substantiate this claim, he begins by returning to the classic Marxist definition of false consciousness – 'they do not know it, but they are doing it'. Where, he inquires, does the ideological mystification lie in this definition – is it in the 'knowing' or in the 'doing'? Initially, the answer to this question seems to be that ideology lies on the side of what people know, or, rather, what they do not know, i.e. people do not *know* what they are doing. They misperceive the reality of their actual situation. As an example of this, Žižek cites the Marxist analysis of commodity fetishism:

> Money is in reality just an embodiment, a condensation, a materialization of a network of social relations – the fact that it functions as a universal equivalent of all commodities is conditioned by its position in the texture of social relations. But to the individuals themselves, this function of money – to be the embodiment of wealth – appears as an immediate, natural property of a thing called 'money'.
>
> (*SOI*: 31)

In other words, money appears to be a direct expression of wealth: you have $10 and I have $5, therefore you are more wealthy than I. However, money in itself is practically worthless, for it is really an indirect expression of the values of different commodities, commodities which, in turn, are the products of the relations of human labour.

The capitalist conception of wealth, for a Marxist, is basically an expression of inequality. It broadly represents the difference between the value of the labour required to make a commodity and the value of the commodity itself. As the latter is inevitably more than the former expressed in monetary terms, it means that the labourers are not paid their full due for the work. In these terms, wealth is really no more than unpaid-for labour. So, instead of expressing a relation between people, people who produce commodities for other people under exploitative conditions, commodities, and ultimately money, appear to express a relation between things, between different amounts of money or commodities. The actual mechanism of society is thereby obscured because the social make-up of labour is hidden behind the circulation of commodities and the money used to pay for them. Therefore those individuals who treat money as if it were inherently valuable are mystified as to its true value. This value lies elsewhere in the relations between the people who make the commodities and those that profit from their labour. Hence, they do not *know* that when they treat money as valuable in itself they are wrong.

As persuasive as this reading of Marx sounds, however, for Žižek it also misses the point that individuals already know that money in itself is not valuable. They are completely aware in their day-to-day use of money that it is only an indirect expression of wealth, that behind the value of money lies a whole complex of social relations. The recent campaigns against Third World 'sweatshops' are an indication of this. Nevertheless, people *act* as if money were inherently valuable. It is this act, an act that continues in spite of the knowledge of its falsity, which, argues Žižek, constitutes the ideological illusion. Ideology, in other words, pertains primarily to the 'doing' rather than the 'knowing'. The illusion or distorted perception of reality is written into the situation itself. I may very well walk around the house all day long reading the works of feminists at the top of my voice, but if I do so while berating my wife for not having my tea on the table or not ironing my shirts on time, I am not a feminist because my *actions* rather than my *knowledge* show me to be an arrant chauvinist.

According to Žižek, what I have overlooked here is not the reality of the situation, but the illusion which structures it. I know full well that women are equal, but I am acting as if I did not. Similarly, I may think that I do not take Nazism seriously, but by attending the Nuremberg rally and saluting Hitler, I show by my actions that I do. I also might claim to be an assiduous supporter of free health care for all, but if I then book myself into a private hospital for treatment in order (so I reason) not to burden the state system, this is a far more convincing demonstration of support for private health care than anything I say. So, to answer the question, it is clear to Žižek that we still are living in an ideological society, it is just that we are fooling ourselves with our cynicism into thinking that we do not take things seriously, whereas in our actions we show effectively that we do. The ideological illusion lies in the reality of what we do, rather than what we think. As such, Žižek is able to rewrite Sloterdijk's formula – 'they know very well what they are doing, but still, they are doing it' – to take account of this – 'they know that, in their activity, they are following an illusion, but still, they are doing it'. We are, as it were, ideologues in practice rather than theory.

BELIEF MACHINES

Perhaps the strangest part of Žižek's formulation here is the implicit proposal that our beliefs or convictions are not what we feel or think, but what we do. What is apparently our most intimate or interior sensation is actually only materialized in our social activity. For Žižek, this is analogous to the way in which Tibetan prayer wheels work. A prayer is inscribed on a piece of paper, rolled up and then placed inside a cylinder which is turned without thinking. The turning of the wheel means that it prays for you or, rather, that you pray via the medium of the wheel. As Žižek points out, it does not matter what you are contemplating when you turn the wheel because, in an objective sense, you are still praying. The sincerity of your prayer, in other words, lies in your action (turning the wheel), and not in what you think.

Žižek's main theoretical reference for the materialization of belief is the French philosopher Blaise Pascal (1623–1662). Pascal is famous for his so-called wager on God. Pascal's wager states that it is more prudent to believe in God because, if you do not, you risk the probability of going to Hell for eternity, which, however small a probability, outweighs all other considerations if it is true:

> Let us weigh up the gain and the loss involved in calling heads that God exists. Let us assess the two cases: if you win you win everything, if you lose you lose nothing. Do not hesitate then; wager that he does exist.
>
> (Pascal 1966: 151)

As Žižek notes, however, this wager is based on reason and argument, the fact that it is only sensible to believe in God. Pascal counters this by proposing that true belief can only come from ritual. When people who did not originally believe in God 'behaved just as if they did believe, taking holy water, having masses said, and so on', Pascal found that they were led to 'believe quite naturally' (Pascal 1966: 152). For Pascal and Žižek, then, the rituals of the Church (in this case the Catholic Church), such as prayer, baptism, mass and so on, are not the expressions of an inner conviction or a pre-existing belief, they are, rather, the pre-text for that belief in the first place. These rituals engender an inner conviction.

In his interpretation of Pascal's theory, Žižek is careful to distinguish between it and what he terms 'the reductionist assertion of the dependence of inner belief on external behaviour' (*MI*: 12). For Žižek, Pascal goes further than merely asserting that the composition of belief is influenced by actual conduct; he argues that by subscribing to the rituals of the Church we believe before we know we do. Our belief is manifest in those rituals – it is staged in advance of our understanding of the fact. When we finally convert to the Church, when we actually believe we believe, all we are doing is recognizing the fact that our belief has already been decided and pre-exists our knowledge of it. Our belief was there objectively all along in the rituals. When we realize this we will believe that when we began to subscribe to these rituals, we began to subscribe to these rituals because of our belief. In other words, the ritual of belief retroactively produces a belief in the ritual. As Žižek comments, Pascal's theory thus describes 'the paradoxical status of a *belief before belief*' (*SOI*: 40).

Such a 'belief before belief' is, like the Tibetan prayer wheel, an automated conviction. It runs, as Pascal describes it, like a machine, ticking over unbeknown to us in our unconscious. For Žižek, the supreme example of such machines in ideology are Ideological State Apparatuses (a term invented by the French Marxist Louis Althusser (1918–1990)) – institutions such as the education system, the Church and the family.

ALTHUSSER'S IDEOLOGICAL STATE APPARATUSES

The term 'Ideological State Apparatus' was coined by Althusser in his influential essay 'Ideology and Ideological State Apparatuses'. Althusser begins this essay by wondering how society reproduces itself; more specifically, he examines the reasons why a capitalist society remains capitalist and does not, for example, lapse into frequent bouts of anarchy and feudalism. What, in other words, compels us to turn up to work every day, rather than setting up independent dictatorships whenever we feel like it? His first answer is that the State has at its disposal large reserves of troops, police and prisons with which it can physically quell any revolt. These reserves belong to what Althusser terms the Repressive State Apparatus. As the title suggests, the Repressive State Apparatus consists of all the ways in which the State can control a population by force. As we saw in the last chapter, for Žižek it is by means of the Repressive State Apparatus – that is by means of physical coercion and violence – that the reign of the law is initially secured.

However, having secured the initialization of the law, how is the law then maintained? In a last resort, the State can always call upon the Repressive

State Apparatus to buttress its authority, such as happens on a micro level with petty crime, and on a macro level with mass demonstrations or revolutions. On a day-to-day basis, though, the State requires a population trained and moulded for its various roles in the Symbolic Order, not one which needs to be prodded out of bed every morning with a bayonet. This, then, for Althusser, is where the Ideological State Apparatuses play their part. The Ideological State Apparatuses are those institutions which help reproduce capitalism by providing it with subjects who are willing to fulfil their role in it. Althusser proposes that the Ideological State Apparatuses are made up of the Churches, the education system, the family unit, the legal system, the political system, trade unions, the communications media and culture. All of these institutions work primarily by means of ideology, rather than by force.

One of the problems with Althusser's Ideological State Apparatuses, however, is precisely the way in which these institutions are supposed to inscribe subjects within ideology. For Althusser this is a matter of what he terms 'interpellation' or 'hailing'. As Althusser proposes, interpellation 'can be imagined along the lines of the most common-place everyday police (or other) hailing: "Hey, you there!"' (quoted in *MI*: 131). In Althusser's model, if you are hailed in this way, you will almost invariably recognize yourself in the call and think that it is precisely you who is being hailed. For Žižek this model of interpellation fails to explain how an Ideological State Apparatus creates belief in an ideology. How is merely being hailed enough to make you believe in ideology? The solution to this problem, according to Žižek, is to view Ideological State Apparatuses as ideology machines in the Pascalian sense. That is, Ideological State Apparatuses are mechanisms which generate a belief in a particular system, creating a conviction in the rectitude of that system before we are even aware of it. They unconsciously pre-empt our belief and thereby habituate us to it.

THE THREE MODES OF IDEOLOGY

If, as Žižek's reading of Althusser seems to show, we can identify the mechanism of ideological belief, does this then mean that we can distinguish ideology from reality? Can we step out of ideology and occupy a non-ideological realm? In order to answer this question, Žižek splits his appraisal of ideology into three parts: *doctrine*, *belief* and *ritual*. These three aspects of ideology correspond to Hegel's tripartite analysis of religion (religion being, for Marx, the supreme example of ideology):

- Doctrine – ideological doctrine concerns the ideas, theories and beliefs of an ideology. For example, the doctrine of liberalism was (partly) originally developed in the ideas of the English philosopher John Locke (1632–1704).
- Belief – ideological belief designates the material or external manifestations and apparatuses of its doctrine. For example, the doctrine of liberalism is materialized in an independent press, democratic elections and the free market.
- Ritual – ideological ritual refers to the internalization of a doctrine, the way it is experienced as spontaneous or natural. In the case of liberalism, for example, subjects spontaneously or naturally think of themselves as free individuals.

These three aspects of ideology form a kind of narrative. In the first stage of ideological doctrine we find ideology in its 'pure' state. Here ideology takes the form of a supposedly truthful proposition or set of arguments which, in reality, conceal a vested interest. Locke's arguments about government, for example, served the interest of the revolutionary Americans rather than the colonizing British. In a second step, a successful ideology takes on the material form which generates belief in that ideology, most potently, as we have seen, in the guise of Ideological State Apparatuses. Third, ideology assumes an almost spontaneous existence, becoming instinctive rather than realized either as an explicit set of arguments or as an institution. The supreme example of such spontaneity is, for Žižek, the notion of commodity fetishism.

In each of these three aspects of the ideological narrative, Žižek identifies the same difficulty in distinguishing between ideology and reality. For example, in the case of doctrine, the idea that we can criticize the truth value of a proposition or set of arguments from a neutral or objective position is, itself, the most fundamental argument of ideology. Such a model is based upon what might be termed a 'common sense' view of epistemology, one which distinguishes between what is true and what is false. It presupposes that if you are able to subject a belief to an ideological critique, you occupy the position of truth or reality, and the belief you are critiquing occupies the position of falsity or ideology. Nowhere is this falsehood more apparent than in the thesis with which this chapter began which states that we now live in a post-ideological age. It is only a post-ideological age from the point of view of capitalism because it no longer has to compare itself with communism. From the point of view of communism, the current age of capitalist domination is thoroughly ideological. As Žižek suggests, even an appeal to the bare facts of a case fails to take account of the ideological horizon in which those facts are understood:

> When a racist Englishman says 'there are too many Pakistanis on our streets!' *how – from what place – does he 'see' this* – that is, how is his symbolic space structured so that he can perceive the fact of a Pakistani strolling along a London street as a disturbing surplus?

> (*TZR*: 64–65)

The answer to this question is that the racist – as with all of us – sees the facts from the viewpoint of a specific Symbolic Order. The Order of the Real contains no excesses or lacks; it is only with the Symbolization of the Real, which is the only Real we have access to, that a surplus of Pakistanis can actually exist. Thus we cannot dissuade someone from a racist ideology by appealing to the facts of a situation because that appeal will equally be limited by its ideological horizon in the Symbolic Order.

Are we therefore condemned to abandoning reality because every access we have to it is ideological? And if we are, might we not as well abandon the concept of ideology itself, given that it now applies to everything and is therefore so all-consuming as to be useless as an analytical tool? The answer, according to Žižek, is 'No', because such a move is itself the supreme ideological gesture. For if we give up the hope of finding a place from which to critique ideology, we are effectively submitting to the inevitability of the ideological. Žižek therefore proposes that there is a place in which we can distinguish the ideological from the non-ideological but it is a place that must remain empty – it is, as it were, a form without a content. What Žižek means by this enigmatic formulation can be understood via an analysis of the spectral supplement of reality.

THE SPECTRE THAT HAUNTS REALITY

So far in this chapter, we have been looking at the question of an ideological critique in a purely binary way: either a viewpoint belongs to ideology or it belongs to reality. Either you understand the truth of a situation or your understanding is skewed. What Žižek contends is that this binary structure misrepresents what is, in fact, a ternary structure. His starting point for this contention is the work of Schelling. According to Žižek, Schelling argues that any organic whole is not made up of two complementary halves, such as inside/outside, life/death or body/spirit, but is rather composed of these two halves plus a double supplement that disturbs the organic whole. So, in the case of body/spirit, for example, there is a spiritual aspect to corporeality, such as that assumed under the guise of animal magnetism, and there is also a corporeal aspect to spirituality, such as the materialization of ghosts. Equally, in terms of the opposition life/death, Žižek argues that this is supplemented by the living death of those who dwell outside the Symbolic, bodies persisting only in the madness of the Real, and it is also supplemented by the deathly life of the Symbolic machine itself which 'behaves as if it possesses a life of its own' (*TPOF*: 89) even though it does not. If this sounds a long way from the analysis of ideology, Žižek suggests that we can witness the effects of these surpluses in commodity fetishism and Ideological State Apparatuses. In terms of commodity fetishism, the 'body' of the commodity is 'spiritualized' in so far as its value is always elsewhere – in other commodities and, ultimately, the labour power which produced it. In terms of Ideological State Apparatuses, they give 'body' to the 'spirit' of ideology, providing an ideological doctrine with a material substance.

THE TWO DEATHS

The fact that, for Žižek, the apparently all-inclusive whole of life and death is supplemented, by both a living death and a deathly life, points to the way in which we can die not just once, but twice. Most obviously, we will suffer a biological death in which our bodies will fail and eventually disintegrate. This is death in the Real, involving the obliteration of our material selves. But we can also suffer a Symbolic death. This does not involve the annihilation of our actual bodies; rather it entails the destruction of our

Symbolic universe and the extermination of our subject positions. We can thus suffer a living death where we are excluded from the Symbolic and no longer exist for the Other. This might happen if we go mad or if we commit an atrocious crime and society disowns us. In this scenario, we still exist in the Real but not in the Symbolic. Alternatively, we might endure a deathly life or more a kind of life after death. This might happen if, after our bodies have died, people remember our names, remember our deeds and so on. In this scenario, we continue to exist in the Symbolic even though we have died in the Real.

The gap between the two deaths, Žižek argues, can be filled either by manifestations of the monstrous or the beautiful. For example, in *Hamlet*, the play by the English dramatist William Shakespeare (1564–1616), Hamlet's father is dead in the Real. However, he persists as a terrifying and monstrous apparition because he was murdered and thereby cheated of the chance to settle his Symbolic debts. Once that debt has been repaid, following Hamlet's killing of his murderer, he is 'completely' dead. Correspondingly, in *Antigone*, the play by the Greek dramatist Sophocles (approx. 496–406 BC), Antigone suffers a Symbolic death before her Real death when she is excluded from the community for wanting to bury her traitorous brother. This destruction of her social identity instils her character with a sublime beauty. Ironically, of course, Antigone enters the domain between the two deaths *'precisely in order to prevent her brother's second death*: to give him a proper funeral that will secure his eternalization' (*TTS*: 170). That is, she endures a Symbolic death in order that her brother, who has been refused proper burial rites, will not suffer a Symbolic death himself.

Žižek's argument is that it is this pseudo-materiality, this spectral supplement, which constitutes the basis of all ideologies. Furthermore, he avers that reality itself depends on this supplement. As he explains, this concept relies on our understanding the distinction between reality and the Real. We have no access to the Real because our world is always mediated by the Symbolic. Reality, as we know it, therefore, is always Symbolic. However, as we saw in Chapter 1, the Symbolization of the Real is, and *cannot* be, complete. The Symbolic can never saturate the Real and so, consequently, there is always some part of the Real which remains unSymbolized. What cannot be accommodated in the Symbolic produces a fundamental antagonism. It is this part of the Real that returns to haunt reality in the guise of the spectral supplement – see Figure 4.1.

The spectre conceals the piece of the Real which has to be forsaken if reality (in the guise of the Symbolic) is to exist. And it is here, in the spectral supplement, that Žižek locates the foundation or kernel of all ideologies. All of which is another way of saying that reality and ideology are mutually implicated in each other. One cannot exist without the other.

Again, as Žižek himself admits, this might sound rather abstract but he is able to provide a concrete example of the way his theory works in terms of class struggle. For Žižek, the class struggle belongs to the Order of the Real. We do not encounter it directly in reality, but only via its Symbolization. As the class struggle is Real, it forms a blockage in the Symbolic which manifests itself in different attempts to Symbolize it, to recuperate it within reality. These attempts index the *antagonistic* character of the class struggle, by which Žižek means to convey that the class struggle is the constitutive split which forms society. The class struggle is what holds society together, it is our mutual bond, but at the same time it is what prevents society from forming an organic whole, it is what drives a wedge between us all. The very visible absence of class struggle right now is, for Žižek, evidence of a struggle in which one side has (temporarily) won. The class struggle does not objectively exist – we can only see it or not see it from a particular, subjective or ideological point of view.

In terms of Žižek's theory, then, the spectre of ideology conceals the failed Symbolization of the antagonism of class struggle in the Real. To put it another way, ideology fills out the abyss of the antagonism – it patches over the hole in reality (the Symbolic Order). Ideology, as it were, makes sense of what does not make sense. For example,

**Spectre of Ideology
concealing gap in
Symbolic**

Reality (the Symbolic)   **Reality (the Symbolic)**

....
The Real (Antagonism)

Figure 4.1 The structure of ideology

Žižek contends that the constitutive antagonism of society is very often made sense of by interpreting it as a complementary pair of opposites. Typical of such a procedure is what Žižek refers to as the New Age reading of the universe in terms of a 'cosmic' pairing – like *yin* and *yang*, or male and female – where any antagonism is held to be the result of an imbalance. Such a reading obscures the fact that, for Žižek, the universe is constitutively unbalanced.

All of which brings us back to the question with which we started the chapter: how can we distinguish reality from ideology? From what position is Žižek able to denounce the New Age reading of the universe as ideological mystification? It is not from a position in reality (you probably will not be surprised to learn!) because, as we have seen, reality is constituted by the Symbolic and the Symbolic is where fiction assumes the guise of truth. The only non-ideological position available is, in fact, in the Real – the Real of the antagonism. As was noted earlier, this is not a position we can actually occupy; it is rather 'the extra-ideological point of reference that authorizes us to denounce the content of our immediate experience as "ideological"' (*MI*: 25). In other words, the antagonism of the Real is a constant that has to be assumed given the existence of social reality (the Symbolic Order). As this antagonism is part of the Real it is not subject to ideological mystification; rather its effect is visible in ideological mystification. Regardless of whether we agree on any particular ideological analysis, therefore, what must be presupposed to exist is the form of ideology itself.

All of which means that the distinction between reality and ideology exists for Žižek as a theoretical given. He does not claim that he can offer any access to the 'objective' truth of things but that ideology must be assumed to exist if we grant that reality is structured upon a constitutive antagonism. And if ideology exists we must be able to subject it to critique. This, then, is ultimately the aim of Žižek's theory of ideology – it is an attempt to keep the project of ideological critique alive at all in an era in which we are said to have left ideology behind. As he emphasizes time and again, the problem with contemporary politics is that it is non-political, that it accepts as natural the existing capitalist structure of society. The first step towards changing this structure is to recognize its 'naturalness' as an ideological formation ripe for critique. The first step towards establishing such a critique is to establish the viability of that critique, and that, finally, is what Žižek's model attempts to do.

SUMMARY

For Žižek, we are not so much living in a post-ideological era as an era dominated by the ideology of cynicism. Adapting the formulas of both Marx and Sloterdijk, Žižek sums up the cynical attitude as 'they know that, in their activity, they are following an illusion, but still, they are doing it'. Ideology, in this sense, is located in what we do and not what we know. Our belief in an ideology is therefore staged in advance of our acknowledging that belief in 'belief machines', such as Althusser's Ideological State Apparatuses.

 Žižek also distinguishes three moments in the narrative of an ideology. These three moments are its explicit proposal in the form of a doctrine, its materialization in the form of belief, and its manifestation as quasi-spontaneous ritual. In each of these three moments, Žižek argues that as soon as we think we have assumed a position of truth from which to denounce the lie of an ideology, we find ourselves back in ideology again. This is because our understanding of ideology is based on binary structure which contrasts reality with ideology. As a solution to this problem, Žižek suggests that we analyse ideology using a triangular or ternary structure. In this model, ideology takes the form of the spectral supplement to reality, concealing the gap opened up by the failure of reality (the Symbolic) to account fully for the Real. While this model of the structure of reality does not allow us a position from which to assume an objective point of view, it does presuppose the existence of ideology and therefore authorizes the validity of its critique.

5

WHAT IS THE RELATIONSHIP BETWEEN MEN AND WOMEN?

THE FORMULAE OF SEXUATION

Undoubtedly the most controversial area of Lacan's psychoanalytic theory is his 'formulae of sexuation'. These formulae – perhaps unhelp-fully compressed into the following slogans: 'Woman does not exist', 'Woman is a symptom of Man', 'there is no sexual relationship' – are concerned to elaborate the gendered structure of the subject using predicate calculus (a form of logic used for exploring the relations between sets). Partly suffering from only approximate translations – in French it is '*la* femme', '*the* Woman', meaning the universal concept of 'woman' – the slogans expressing these formulae seem to suggest that women are somehow inherently lesser beings than men, subsidiary developments of an authentic and masculine humanity. As Lacan was neither very concerned about observing the sanctities of (what we now think of as) political correctness, nor inclined to dissuade people from thinking ill of him by rendering his explanations as transparent as possible, the formulae of sexuation have continued to provoke critics and divide loyalties.

Given his 'dogmatic' Lacanianism, it is little surprise that Žižek numbers himself among those feminists who argue that the formulae of sexuation constitute the most advanced elaboration of the gendered subject. It is perhaps worth pointing out that he argues this case with the same egalitarian confidence with which he argues the case for any Lacanian concept. Žižek explains how these formulae work and puts them to use, but he does not necessarily defend them. In other words, he does not always pay homage to the outraged reception of the formulae. By adopting this approach, which is one not dissimilar to Lacan's own infamous insouciance, it is not always clear where Žižek falls short of gleefully offending the literal-minded. Indeed, there are points in his deliberations when he courts the risk of seeming to list all the received notions of femininity without critique. In an era where theory often spends more time establishing its pious credentials than actually articulating nuanced thought, this tactic no doubt seems refreshingly iconoclastic. Nowhere is such iconoclasm more in evidence than in his discussions of the formulae – discussions which often take as a starting point the notorious anti-feminist and anti-Semitic tract *Sex and Character* by the German philosopher Otto Weininger (1880–1903).

'WOMAN DOES NOT EXIST'

Sex and Character, which was originally shown to Freud in draft form and heavily criticized by him, is an attempt to explain the differences and relationship between the sexes. As it often contains claims about women apparently homologous to Lacan's formulae of sexuation, Žižek uses the book as a kind of sounding board against which he can show up the errors of an utterly misogynist interpretation of the formulae. In Žižek's reading of Weininger, sexual difference is predicated upon an association with the opposition between subject and object. Men are active, noble spirits (or subjects) and women are passive, ignoble matter (or objects). As passive matter, women are ruled by sexuality; indeed, according to Weininger, women are '*sexually affected and penetrated* by every thing' (quoted in *TMOE*: 137). In this regard, coitus is merely a particularly intense example of the general experience of sexuality which defines 'woman'. A woman's personal sexuality is thus just an instance of a universal and impersonal instinct, one which governs her entire behaviour. Even if she tells the truth, she does not tell the truth for the sake of the truth, but to impress a potential mate.

For Weininger, man, on the other hand, is a being torn between his senses and his spirituality, between sexuality and love. However, this presents a problem, for how can a man entertain a spiritual relationship with a woman if she is defined as a being for whom spirituality is completely absent? The answer to this puzzle, according to Weininger, is that the spiritual beauty of a woman (which makes her a fit object for man's love) is actually a product of that love in the first place. Man's love, in other words, functions as a performative. Man projects onto woman an ideal she can never attain, and so, in loving woman, man really loves himself. In fact, man loves the better part of himself, the ideal, spiritual side, rather than the tainted sexual side of his senses. By so doing, man betrays not only himself, because he fails to realize his spiritual potential in himself, but he also betrays woman, because he disregards her empirical actuality, subjecting her to an Imaginary idealism. Thus it is that, for Weininger, 'love is murder' (quoted in *TMOE*: 140).

PERFORMATIVES AND THE GENUS THAT IS ALWAYS ONE OF ITS OWN SPECIES

Žižek often has recourse to the concept of the 'performative' throughout his work, so it is worthwhile knowing what he means by it. The term itself is taken from the work of the British philosopher J.L. Austin (1911–1960) on speech-act theory. Speech-act theory divides language up between 'performatives' and 'constatives'. A constative statement is a statement that describes something, seemingly in terms that can be verified as true or false. For example, 'the house is red' is a constative statement. Performatives, on the other hand, are statements which either *do* something *in* the saying, such as 'I hereby pronounce you husband and wife', or produce an effect *by* the saying, such as convincing you of an argument. In the light of this, we might say that the Symbolic Order is one large performative, as it confers Symbolic efficiency on certain acts, provides you with a role, a lineage, and so on. As Žižek notes by way of an example, 'the meeting is closed when, by means of the utterance, "The meeting is closed," this fact *comes to the big Other's knowledge*' (*EYS*: 98). Indeed, what is striking about Austin's theory is, as Žižek points out, that it concludes that all language is ultimately performative. Even supposedly straightforward constatives, such as 'the house is red', affirm a certain organization of reality or ordering of it.

By asserting that performatives are simultaneously both just *one part* of all speech acts and also *ultimately all* speech acts, Austin enters what Žižek terms the realm of the philosophical. In other words, one of the things that

defines philosophy for Žižek is when one part of a system of thought is privileged as the ground or horizon of meaning for the rest of the system.
Borrowing from Hegel, Žižek summarizes this by stating that 'the genus is
always one of its own species' (*TMOE*: 97). In other words, the universal
concept of something (for example, speech acts) is, for Žižek, always
defined by a particular instance of that concept (in this case, the performative). Another way to look at this is to think that the whole of something
(all speech acts) can only be realized by unbalancing that whole with an
excess (by stating that all speech acts are ultimately performatives, even
though some of these performatives are also constatives). Therein resides
the meaning of Žižek's repeated discussions of the word 'and' in the titles
of philosophers' works. Where an 'and' appears in such a title or statement
it signifies a relationship between part and whole in which one element
of the whole forms the ground for the rest of the whole. For example,
when Marx refers to 'the exclusive realm of Freedom, Equality, Property
and Bentham' (Marx 1976: 280), the last term – 'Bentham' – is the horizon
of meaning in which we should read the other terms. As Žižek argues, 'the
supplementary "Bentham" stands for the social circumstances that provide
the concrete content of the pathetic phrases on freedom and equality –
commodity exchange, market bargaining, utilitarian egotism' (*TIR*: 104). In
Marx's statement, then, 'Bentham' functions as a *point de capiton*, pinning
down the rest of the words in the sentence. Similarly, we might say that
the whole of Žižek's work is predicated upon Lacanian psychoanalysis,
Hegelian philosophy and Marxist political economy, but that this whole
finds its horizon of meaning (or *point de capiton*) in one part of that
whole – Marxist political economy. Marxist political economy, in other
words, is the element of the whole (of Žižek's work) that overflows, or is in
excess of, all the other elements of that whole.

Given that it is a calamity for all concerned, why therefore does
man continue to misrecognize his spiritual ideal in woman by choosing
her as his love-object? The solution to this problem advanced by
Weininger is that man's descent into sexuality creates woman in the
first place. Reversing the biblical narrative which avows that it is
woman who causes the sin of mankind, Weininger boldly proposes
that '*woman is the sin of man*' (quoted in *TMOE*: 141). She is produced
by man and exists only in so far as man embraces his own sexuality
at the expense of his spirituality. It is thus unsurprising that woman's

one aim is to perpetuate the sexuality of man, because if she did not she would not exist. Woman is just an effect; in herself *'woman therefore does not exist'* (quoted in *TMOE*: 141). All of which explains why man chooses woman as his privileged love-object: as it is man's 'fault' that woman exists in the first place, he is wracked by guilt at his crime and strives to placate that guilt by loving her. Nevertheless, however much man loves woman and she strives to internalize the spiritual values of man, she cannot escape her true nature. For Weininger, woman is inherently unfree, a slave to the Phallus (or patriarchal law) who, if she attempts to repress this fact, will suffer from hysteria when her true nature fights back.

As is clear from this summary, then, Weininger's theory is probably one of the most candid statements of misogyny ever published. For Žižek, however, it is precisely this frankness, the extremity of Weininger's views, which means that *Sex and Character* unwittingly provides a basis for a Lacanian feminism. The first point of note, in this regard, is that Weininger dispenses with any notion of woman as 'enigmatic', of femininity as a 'dark secret' inaccessible to the light of reason. For, on the contrary, Weininger thoroughly dissects the notion of femininity and finds that, after all, there is nothing there. The secret of woman is that she does not exist. Having accomplished this break from traditional, patriarchal descriptions of woman as the mysterious or enigmatic limit of male reason, Weininger, for Žižek, fails to go far enough. He fails to recognize in the 'nothingness' he discerns in woman, the very basis of subjectivity itself.

As we saw in Chapter 1, the subject is precisely this void or nothingness that precedes its inscription within the Symbolic Order. What Weininger fears, according to Žižek, is not woman, but the void of subjectivity itself, the absolute negativity of the 'night of the world' which forms the subject. Woman, in other words, is the subject par excellence. The fact that behind the enigma, the feminine mask, Weininger does not find *something* – some opaque mystery – but, rather, *nothing*, means that, for Žižek, Weininger stumbled accidentally upon the universal truth of subjectivity. Another way of looking at this is to conceive of it in terms of the distinction borrowed from linguistics by Lacan between the subject of the *enunciation* and the subject of the *enunciated*. The abyss or void of subject is the subject of enunciation, whereas the subject of the enunciated is the Symbolic subject, the subject of the social network. Weininger's contention that

THE SUBJECT OF THE ENUNCIATION AND THE SUBJECT OF THE ENUNCIATED

The subject of the enunciation (or *énonciation*) is the 'I' who speaks, the individual doing the speaking; the subject of the enunciated (or *énoncé* – called by some critics 'the subject of the statement') is the 'I' of the sentence, the grammatical designation or pronoun used by all individuals. 'I', in other words, is not identical to itself – it is split between the individual 'I' (the subject of the enunciation) and the grammatical 'I' (the subject of the enunciated). Although we may experience them as unified, this is merely an Imaginary illusion, for the abstract pronoun 'I' is actually a substitute or a stand-in for the 'I' of the subject. It does not account for me in my full specificity; it is, rather, a general term I share with everyone else. In order to share it with everyone else, my empirical reality must, in a sense, be annihilated or, as Lacan dramatically avers, 'the symbol manifests itself first of all as the murder of the thing' (Lacan 1977: 104). In other words, the subject can only enter language by negating the Real, 'murdering' or substituting the blood-and-sinew reality of self for the concept of the self expressed in words – in names or pronouns, for example. For Lacan and Žižek, therefore, every word is a gravestone, marking the absence or corpse of the thing it represents and standing in for it. It is partly in the light of this that Lacan is boldly able to refashion Descartes' 'I think, therefore, I am' as 'I think where I am not, therefore I am where I do not think' (Lacan 1977: 166). The 'I think' here is the subject of the enunciated (the Symbolic subject), whereas the 'I am' is the subject of the enunciation (the Real subject). What Lacan aims to disclose by rewriting the Cartesian *cogito* in this way is that the subject is irrevocably split, torn asunder by language.

'woman does not exist' therefore amounts to saying that woman does not exist at the level of the subject of the enunciated – she is excluded from Weininger's patriarchal Symbolic – she only exists at the level of the enunciation, as the void of the subject.

'WOMAN IS A SYMPTOM OF MAN'

We can perhaps see now how Žižek pushes the logic of Weininger's theory to the extreme in order to demonstrate that 'woman does not exist' in so far as she is the subject in its modality of absolute negativity. Nevertheless, how does he then escape what he admits is the apparently obvious parallel between Weininger's assertion that man creates woman and Lacan's formula 'woman is a symptom of man'? The first point Žižek makes in this regard is to note that Lacan's thesis is a product of his later work. This chronological point is important because Lacan fundamentally changed his concept of the symptom from his first articulation of it in the 1950s to his last reformulation of it in the 1970s. In the earlier theory, a symptom is a cipher or a message which returns to the subject the truth about his desire, a desire that was betrayed.

If woman is a symptom in this sense then she is merely an embodiment of the betrayal of man's desire, the fact that man 'gave way as to his desire' (*EYS*: 154). There is therefore little difference between this notion and Weininger's contention that when man fails to fulfil his spiritual potential (his true desire), this failure manifests itself in the creation of woman (as a symptom). As soon as man recognizes this failure and returns to the truth of his desire to be a spiritual being, woman will disappear. She only exists as a result of the unethical division in man himself and therefore has no existence in her own right. In his readings of the operas of the German composer Richard Wagner (1813–1883), Žižek proposes that there is what he terms a 'Wagnerian performative' which functions to the same kind of logic espoused by Weininger. When, by means of a performative, a Wagnerian hero fulfils his Symbolic role, this action 'proves incompatible with the very being of woman' (*EYS*: 155). In *The Flying Dutchman*, for example, as a result of the captain finally proclaiming that he is the 'flying Dutchman', Senta kills herself. Žižek argues that a similar pattern emerges in hard-boiled detective fiction and *film noir*. In the *noir* universe woman appears as a materialization of the detective's ceding of his ethical desire to discover the truth – he is not so much side-tracked by woman (in the guise of the *femme fatale*) as woman embodies his being side-tracked. When the detective returns to his desire and, as it were, stays true to himself, the woman invariably disappears or dies, both of which happen, for example, to Velma/Grayle in *Farewell, My Lovely*, by the American author Raymond Chandler (1888–1959), after Marlowe confronts her with the truth.

In contrast to this theory, and the readings produced by it, 'woman as a symptom of man' refers to Lacan's later concept of the symptom.

In order to differentiate it from earlier conceptions, such a symptom is sometimes referred to by Lacan and Žižek using the neologism *sinthome*. In this case, the symptom or *sinthome* is the signifying formation in which an individual subject organizes its relationship to enjoyment, or *jouissance*. Enjoyment, or *jouissance*, is to be distinguished from mere pleasure. It is the pleasure beyond mere pleasure itself – a pleasure that has an orgasmic charge, indexing the point where pleasure becomes pain. As such it expresses the kind of satisfaction to be garnered from picking at your own festering wound, a wound which, Žižek advises us, neatly symbolizes the notion of symptom. The symptom is just such a wound in the subject, one which bestows upon the subject its consistency. As Žižek avers, the *sinthome* is

> a particular, 'pathological', signifying formation, a binding of enjoyment, an inert stain resisting communication and interpretation, a stain which cannot be included in the circuit of discourse, of social bond network, but is at the same time a positive condition of it.
>
> (*SOI*: 75)

As an example of such a stain Žižek cites the alien in the film *Alien*. While it is a supplement to the crew in the drifting spaceship, it is also what, by virtue of its threat to them, confers a unity upon the group. Indeed, the ambiguous relationship we maintain towards our symptoms – one in which we enjoy our suffering and suffer our enjoyment – is exemplified by the way in which the Ripley character (played by Sigourney Weaver) has progressively come to identify with the alien as the film series has developed.

It should perhaps be clearer now that what Žižek means when he refers to the formula 'woman is the symptom of man' is not the same as Weininger's contention that woman depends for her existence on man. In fact, quite the opposite is the case. For if the symptom is what maintains the consistency of the subject, equally its dissolution will betray that consistency and the subject will disappear. Therefore, the thesis that 'woman is the symptom of man' registers the fact that man only exists in so far as woman confers consistency upon him. Man, in other words, depends for his existence on woman. His being is external to himself. He 'literally *ex-sists*', as Žižek avers, 'his entire being lies "out there," in woman' (*EYS*: 155). So, despite the similarity between the Lacanian slogan – 'woman is a symptom of man' – and Weininger's thesis, which Žižek deploys as a kind of worse-case scenario reading of that slogan, the meaning of the two statements are diametrically opposed.

'THERE IS NO SEXUAL RELATIONSHIP'

However, at best, are we not left here with a reversal of terms, one which is actually misandrist (displaying a denigration of men) rather than misogynist? Or, at worst, is not Žižek reinforcing Weininger's designation of woman as a passive object, one that here manifests itself in its most ancient form, depicting woman as the passive receptacle or carrier of man's innate being? In order to dispel these conceptions, it is probably apposite at this stage to confirm that when Žižek writes about 'man' and 'woman' these terms are not to be understood as expressing an essentialist point of view. In other words, the term 'man' does not necessarily refer to someone with a penis, just as the term 'woman' does not necessarily refer to someone with a vagina.

If many people might find such an assertion hard to accept, many others might well understand this to indicate the prevalence of two 'cosmic' poles – the masculine and the feminine – both of which are shared by men and women. After all, we are now familiar with the concept of men trying to 'discover their feminine side' and vice versa. The whole notion of equality between the sexes is often based on the principle of a kind of balance, the fact that we are able to deploy different aspects of ourselves in different situations and that no one sex is therefore able to monopolize any particular activity. However, this is not what Žižek means by 'man' and 'woman'. Nor does he mean by it a variation on this theme, such as may be found in the best-selling book *Men are from Mars, Women are from Venus* by the American author John Gray (b. 1951), which finds that men and women are (metaphorically) from different planets with different (and therefore misunderstood) psychic economies. Rather, the problem for men and women is, according to Žižek, that we both come '*from the same planet which is, as it were, split from within*' (*TTS*: 272).

In order to explain this assertion and thus understand what Žižek means by 'woman' and 'man', we need to attend to the slogan which sits at the heart of the Lacanian formulae of sexuation: 'there is no sexual relationship'. I will not reproduce the formulae here using the form of calculus that Lacan deploys but, instead, summarize its main points in a simplified format in Table 5.1. What probably first strikes someone about these formulae is that the validity of one formula (for example, 'all speaking beings are subject to the phallic function') renders impossible the coexistence of another formula (for example, 'not all speaking beings are subject to the phallic function). This impossibility is already one way of interpreting the slogan 'there is no sexual relationship', in the sense that there is no way of establishing any harmony between the four positions elaborated here.

To get beyond such an innocent reading of the formulae, we have to understand what is meant by the 'phallic function'. At a basic level, the phallic function represents (somewhat paradoxically given its name) the function of castration. Let me be clear here: neither Lacan nor Žižek are talking about severing actual penises. In fact, they are not talking about actual penises at all. As the title 'phallus' suggests, their point of reference here is a symbol. Castration is merely the name given to the process by which we enter the Symbolic Order, the process by which we substitute the actual thing for a symbol of that thing. In this sense, castration signifies the loss engendered by the process of Symbolization. As Lacan's reworking of the Cartesian *cogito* suggests – 'I think where I am not, therefore I am where I do not think' – when we choose thought we lose being, when we choose words we murder the things which they represent. In line with this, what we also lose with the advent of castration is *jouissance*. It is subject to a Symbolic prohibition, a prohibition signified by the phallus.

If we now turn to the gendered differences between the various relations towards the phallic function, we can see (in Formula 2) that all men are defined by the fact that they must submit to symbolic castration. In the kind of paradox which, by now, is probably familiar to Žižekian converts, this universal rule can only be established by an

Table 5.1 The formulae of sexuation

Man	Woman
Formula 1 There is a speaking being that says 'no' to the phallic function	Formula A There is no speaking being that says 'no' to the phallic function
Formula 2 All speaking beings are subject to the phallic function	Formula B Not all speaking beings are subject to the phallic function

exception to it – the man (in Formula 1) who does not have to sacrifice his *jouissance*. This, for Žižek, is 'the primordial father of the Freudian myth in *Totem and Taboo*, a mythical being who has had all women and was capable of achieving complete satisfaction' (*FTKN*: 123). The mythical status of this man is important, for he has to be dead or indeed slaughtered in order for men in general to persist in the Symbolic. His myth sustains the illusion necessary to the Symbolic that the full plenitude of *jouissance* will once again be available.

In the status of this exception that guarantees the totality, we can perhaps see an analogy with the thesis that 'the genus is always one of its own species'. In addition to all men, there is a Man who sustains them. It is similar to the way in which, for the ancients, in addition to the four elements or essences that made up the universe – earth, water, air, and fire – there was a fifth element, the *quintessence* as it was called, which was actually latent in all things. The man with complete access to *jouissance* is, in this sense, quintessential to the universality of castrated men. In contrast to this, which is why I have not labelled the formulae sequentially, the logic of woman belongs to the 'not-all'. If, as we have seen, the whole of man, the set of all men, is only defined by granting an exception to that set (in Formula 1), then, conversely, the fact that under the designation 'woman' there is no exception to the phallus – 'there is no speaking being that says 'no' to the phallic function' (in Formula A) – means that woman is not a totality, or a whole: she is, in other words, not-all. The exception in the formula for man, which Žižek identifies with the primal father of *Totem and Taboo*, functions as a limit or boundary against which man as a whole is defined, but this is not granted woman – there is no limit or boundary to woman. So, whereas the primal father embodies the concept of Man ('Man' with a capital 'M', as opposed to all men, counted one by one), there is no equivalent universal notion of Woman. This then, finally, is what is meant by 'woman does not exist': *la femme*, *the* Woman does not exist.

What this means is that there is a 'feminine resistance to symbolic identification' (*TWTN*: 57). Žižek proposes that the form this resistance takes is hysterical. Hysteria, for psychoanalysis at least, designates an attitude of questioning, specifically a questioning of the big Other. Such questioning in Žižek's work is often rendered in shorthand as '*Che vuoi?*' – 'What does the big Other want from me?' By its very articulation, this question creates a distance between the questioner and the big Other, the Symbolic Order. It thus designates the failure of the Symbolic Order, but – and this is crucial – it also designates the moment of subjectivity. If we completely assume our position in the Symbolic and take up our role in it 100 per cent, what part of us, as subjects, is actually subjective? The answer is that no part of us is – we would be wholly subsumed in the Symbolic, wholly objective. Our status as subjects, as subjective beings, issues directly from our failure to integrate fully in the Symbolic. The failure of the Symbolic is, therefore, strictly correlative with the creation of subjectivity. The subject is precisely that part of us which disassociates itself from the big Other in the form of the hysteric's *'Che vuoi?'* – the questioning of the Symbolic.

From this theory we may surmise two things: first, that the status of the subject is inherently hysterical and, second, that woman, as the hysterical being, is the authentic subject. This, finally, is where Žižek locates the value of Weininger's *Sex and Character*. What this text represents is the culmination of a trend beginning in the late nineteenth century – a trend in which 'the sudden emergence of the figure of the hysterical woman (in the works of Richard Wagner, Franz Kafka, Edvard Munch, and others) announced a crisis of sexual relationship in whose shadow we continue to live' (*GAV*: 2). The horror expressed by Wagner's operas, Kafka's stories or Munch's paintings at the hysteria of women is merely the horror of recognition – the recognition that (all along) at the heart of the subject there is nothing, the 'nothing' which is precisely the failure of Symbolization. Man, in the formulae of sexuation, is what fills out this 'nothing'. In other words, woman is the limit of the abyss against which man defines himself. What the designations 'man' and 'woman' represent, therefore, are two modes of the failure of Symbolization. 'Woman' and 'man' are not biological givens, they are not subject positions or roles which we assume, rather, they are the two ways in which the failure of Symbolization is given form.

This, then, is what 'there is no sexual relationship' means. It does not mean that in *reality* there is no such thing as sex or coitus. Rather, it refers to a more profound distress, which is that sexual difference is Real and that, as such, it is impossible to Symbolize. In a similar way to which, for Žižek, class conflict is an expression of an antagonism in the Real, so 'man' and 'woman' are failed attempts to transpose the Real of sexual difference into Symbolic oppositions. The difference between the sexes, therefore, is not a simple question of assuming two different Symbolic mandates – these are not roles as such, failure to fulfil either of which means that you are expelled into the Real. Instead, the designations 'man' and 'woman' refer to different ways to account for the failure to Symbolize the Real of sexual difference.

The American feminist Judith Butler (b. 1956) has queried this theory and asked if it means that 'feminism is a dead end' (*CHU*: 6). For if sexual difference is Real, does that not mean it is, in some way, transcendental or a 'natural given'? And if sexual difference is 'naturally given' surely any attempt to improve the present conditions of women can always be trumped by reference to 'the way things really are'? The answer to both these questions, for Žižek, is 'no'. Such arguments, he claims, rely on a kind of temporal confusion in which the Real is only understood as being prior to the Symbolic, whereas the Real is actually produced by the failure of the Symbolic. The Real is what is left over after Symbolization and, as Symbolization changes through history, feminism is therefore not a pointless exercise in trying to change what cannot be changed. Indeed, far from there being a given set of norms against which we can judge people, Žižek contends that there are no norms as such:

> It is not that we have homosexuals, fetishists, and other perverts *in spite of* the normative fact of sexual difference – that is, as proofs of the failure of sexual difference to impose its norm; it is not that sexual difference is the ultimate point of reference which anchors the contingent drifting of sexuality; it is, on the contrary, on account of the gap which forever persists between the real of sexual difference and the determinate forms of heterosexual symbolic norms that we have the multitude of 'perverse' forms of sexuality.
>
> (*TTS*: 273)

Our sexuality, then, is a strange combination of what Žižek refers to as 'animal coupling' (*EYS*: 154) – the biological fact of copulation regulated by instinct and natural rhythms – onto which is grafted the Symbolic deadlock of the impossibility of sexual difference. These two elements – animal coupling and the failure of Symbolization – are not linked in any way except by their contingent encounter at the level of our sexuality. Our sexuality, in other words, is the product of the entanglement of the living body in the Symbolic Order. There is not a perfect 'fit' between the two because if there were the Symbolic

Order would not actually exist. It is predicated upon its own insufficiency, its inability to complete itself or conform to a perfect fit between the world of things and the world of words. And it is precisely the Symbolic's insufficiency which is referred to in the slogan 'there is no sexual relationship'.

As a final sting in the tail, Žižek suggests that the fact that 'there is no sexual relationship' is precisely why we have love. According to Žižek, 'love is a lure, a mirage, whose function is to obfuscate the irreducible, constitutive "out-of-joint" of the relationship between the sexes' (*GAV*: 2). In this sense, love is akin to ideology; we may even say that it *is* the ideology of sexual difference. For in the same way that the spectre of ideology conceals the failed Symbolization of class struggle in the Real, so love conceals the failed Symbolization of sexual difference. Indeed, love at its most beguiling, such as may be found in the detective's love for the *femme fatale*, presents a series of obstacles to its own fulfilment. These obstacles merely obscure the fact that the fulfilment which they seem to hinder is not actually possible – that, in the end, it is not possible to reconcile 'man' with 'woman'.

SUMMARY

Many of Žižek's discussions of the differences between men and women refer to Otto Weininger's book *Sex and Character*. In this book, Weininger proposes that women are created by men's failure to fulfil their own spiritual potential. As such, Weininger's theory sounds very close to Lacan's formulae of sexuation which, in the form of slogans, propose that 'woman is a symptom of man' and that 'woman does not exist'. In other words, Weininger's theory represents an extreme misreading of the formulae. For Žižek, however, these formulae mean that woman is what sustains the consistency of man, and that woman's non-existence actually represents the radical negativity which constitutes all subjects. The terms 'man' and 'woman' do not, for Žižek, refer to a biological distinction or gender roles, but rather two modes of the failure of Symbolization. It is this failure which means that 'there is no sexual relationship'.

6

WHY IS RACISM
ALWAYS A FANTASY?

'CHE VUOI?': 'WHAT DO YOU WANT FROM ME?'

For Žižek, racism begins with the question of '*Che vuoi?*'. As we saw in Chapter 5, '*Che vuoi?*' is a shorthand way of asking 'What do you want from me?'. This question arises from the arbitrary character of our roles in the Symbolic Order. These roles are arbitrary in that they are not the direct consequence of our actual, real properties. For example, if I am a king there is nothing inherently 'kingly' about me; I do not have an intrinsic quality of 'kingliness' that I am born with. The qualities of 'kingliness' are conferred upon me by my position in the Symbolic Order when I am born into a royal family. We therefore maintain a distance towards our roles because we do not feel we can fully account for them. This distance is expressed by the '*Che vuoi?*' – '*Why am I what you say I am?*' – the question we address to the big Other. It is a question asked these days less by kings and more by celebrities: do you (the fans) love me for my fame (my role in the Symbolic Order) or for who I really am?

What, however, has this to do with racism? According to Žižek the question of '*Che vuoi?*' or what you really want from me 'erupts most violently in the purest, so to say distilled form of racism, in anti-Semitism: in the anti-Semitic perspective, the Jew is precisely a person about whom it is never clear "what he really wants"' (*SOI*: 114).

As is suggested here, the Jew is the paradigmatic figure of the victim of racism for Žižek. Elsewhere, he concedes that this figure may well be Afro-American or Japanese, but in Europe the Jew has always been *the* subject of racism. The Jew is suspicious because we do not know what he wants – his intentions and his desires are unclear to us. In order to dissipate our own sense of incomprehension thrown up by the Jewish '*Che vuoi?*' we create our own scenario, explaining the Jew's actions in terms of a hidden agenda – 'This is what he *really* wants (to get all our money, to take over the world, etc.)'. This scenario, this answer to the '*Che vuoi?*', is a fantasy. Fantasy functions as an attempt to fill out the void of the question of 'What do you want from me?' by providing us with a tangible answer. It spares us from the perplexity of not knowing what the Other really wants from us.

In order to clarify this point, Žižek suggests that the reason the Jews have become the paradigmatic subjects of racism is because of the particular character of the Jewish God. The Jewish God is unknowable. The Judaic prohibition on making images of God means that, for Žižek, the Jewish God persists as the incarnation of '*Che vuoi?*' – we never really know what He desires from us. Even when this God pronounces a comprehensible order, such as when he demands that Abraham sacrifice his son, it remains unclear what he actually wants from Abraham, what God's intention is behind this command. Abraham's position in this respect is emblematic of the position of the Jews as a whole. Why were they picked by God to be the 'chosen people'? In themselves they were not special, but they became 'the chosen ones' when they assumed their Symbolic mandate, the role that God had chosen for them. The starting point for a Jewish believer is thus the perplexity of the '*Che vuoi?*' – 'What does God want from us?'. In contrast to the anxiety of Judaism, Žižek asserts that Christianity is founded upon the pacification of the '*Che vuoi?*': the Passion of Christ, the image of Christ upon the Cross, is a kind of fantasy scenario which fills in the void of the question of the desire of the Other. By sacrificing His son, God reassures Christian believers that He loves them and thus makes His desire clear.

What Žižek insists we be clear on here is that fantasy, as a psycho-analytic category, is not reducible to an imagined scenario in which our desires are satisfied. The first point to note here is that desire itself cannot be satisfied or fulfilled. In order to exemplify this, Žižek relates the plot of 'Store of the Worlds', the story by American author Robert

HYSTERIA, OBSESSIONAL NEUROSIS AND PERVERSION

We saw in the previous chapter that the question of '*Che vuoi?*' defines the position of hysteria. The hysteric is never clear what the Other wants and is therefore always plagued by a kind of self-doubt, manifest in a recurrent questioning. In straightforward hysteria the subject believes that what the Other wants from him or her is love. In obsessional neurosis, which is a sub-set of hysteria, the subject believes that what the Other wants is work, and so the obsessional devotes him or herself to frenetic activity. Žižek often contrasts these hysterical responses with perversion. Despite its everyday associations with so-called sexual deviancy, perversion is also a technical term that Lacanian psychoanalysis uses to designate a certainty that a subject knows what the Other wants. The pervert is therefore defined by a lack of questioning. He or she is convinced of the meaning of the desire of the Other.

Scheckley (b. 1928), in which the central character visits an old recluse who, it is claimed, can satisfy people's desires by means of a drug. Before commencing with the drug, the old man advises the story's hero, a man called Wayne, to go away and think about what he is going to do. Back with his wife and child, Wayne gets caught up in day-to-day family life. Although he keeps promising himself that he will one day visit the old man and have his inner desires realized, it is a whole year later before he finally decides to go. At this point, however, Wayne suddenly wakes up in the presence of the old man who asks him if he is satisfied. Wayne agrees that he is and scurries off across a landscape devastated by nuclear war. The trick of the story, as Žižek avers, is that 'we mistake for postponement of the "thing itself" what is already the "thing itself", we mistake for the searching and indecision proper to desire what is, in fact, the realization of desire' (*LA*: 7). In other words, the desire realized in fantasy is only 'satisfied' by the postponement of satisfaction, by the perpetuation of desire. As soon as desire is satisfied, in the sense of being fulfilled, it disappears.

The second feature of fantasy that Žižek insists upon is that the object of our desire is not something given in advance. Rather, fantasy teaches us what to desire in the first place. Fantasy actually constitutes our desire, as Žižek explains:

> Fantasy does not mean that when I desire a strawberry cake and cannot get it in reality, I fantasize about eating it; the problem is, rather: *how do I know that I desire a strawberry cake in the first place? This* is what fantasy tells me.

(*TPOF*: 7)

The fantasy of desiring a strawberry cake is my own individual concern. Fantasy, at this level, is very specifically mine. At the same time, however, the desire that is realized in this fantasy is not strictly my desire – it is, rather, the desire of the Other, the desire which throws up the enigma of '*Che vuoi?*'. The question of desire is therefore never directly a matter of what I want, but what the Other wants from me: what I am to other people.

In order to exemplify this, Žižek reports the incident noted by Freud of his daughter's fantasy of eating a strawberry cake. Freud's daughter's fantasy is not just a case of simple wish-fulfilment in which she wanted a strawberry cake and in order to satisfy this desire she dreamt up a scenario in which she ate one. For what is at stake here is not her desire but the desire of the Other, in this case her parents, which permeated her desire. Previously, when eating a strawberry cake with a degree of gusto, Freud's daughter had observed how much her parents seemed to enjoy the scene of her eating. It was thus clear to her what her parents wanted from her – they wanted her to devour strawberry cake. The girl's fantasy of eating strawberry cake was therefore a way of answering the question of '*Che vuoi?*' or 'What do my parents want from me?'. Although the fantasy of the strawberry cake was her fantasy, the desire it realized was actually that of her parents' desire. More precisely, we can say that the desire of Freud's daughter was the desire for the desire of the Other (for the answer to the question of what her parents wanted from her).

Fantasy, then, is what Žižek terms *intersubjective*. What Žižek means by this is that fantasy is only produced by the interaction between subjects. However specific a fantasy is to an individual, that fantasy in itself is always a product of an intersubjective situation. In order to make this clearer we can schematize the relation between '*Che vuoi?*', fantasy and desire in Figure 6.1.

FANTASY AS A MASK OF THE INCONSISTENCY IN THE BIG OTHER

Another way of looking at the relationship between fantasy and the big Other which Žižek often alludes to is to think of fantasy as concealing the inconsistency of the Symbolic Order. In order to understand this we need to know why the big Other is inconsistent, or structured around a gap. The answer to this question, according to Žižek, is that when the body enters the field of signification or the big Other, it is castrated. What Žižek means by this is that the price we pay for our admission to the universal medium of language is the loss of our full bodily selves. When we submit to the big Other we sacrifice direct access to our bodies and, instead, are condemned to an indirect relation with it via the medium of language. So, whereas before we enter language we are what Žižek terms 'pathological' subjects (the subject he notates by the figure 'S'), after we are immersed in language we are what he refers to as 'barred' subjects (the empty subject he notates with the figure '$'). What is barred from the barred subject is precisely the body as the materialization, or incarnation, of enjoyment. Material enjoyment is strictly at odds with, or heterogeneous to, the immaterial order of the signifier.

In order for the subject to enter the Symbolic Order, then, the Real of enjoyment or *jouissance* has to be evacuated from it. Which is another way of saying that, as we saw in the previous chapter, the advent of the symbol entails 'the murder of the thing'. Although not all enjoyment is completely evacuated by the process of signification (some of it persists in what we call erogenous zones), most of it is not Symbolized. What this means is that the Symbolic Order cannot fully account for enjoyment – it is what is missing from the big Other. The big Other is therefore inconsistent or structured around a lack, the lack of enjoyment. It is, we might say, castrated or rendered incomplete by admitting the subject, in much the same way as the subject is castrated by its admission.

What fantasy does is conceal this lack or incompletion. So, for example, as we saw in the previous chapter, 'there is no sexual relationship' in the big Other. What the fantasy of a sexual scenario thereby conceals is the impossibility of this sexual relationship. It covers up the lack in the big Other, the missing *jouissance*. In this regard, Žižek often avers that fantasy is a way for subjects to organize their *jouissance* – it is a way to manage or domesticate the traumatic loss of the enjoyment which cannot be Symbolized.

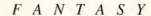

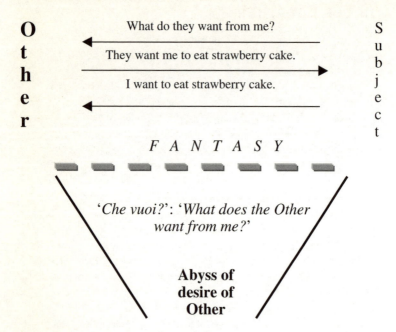

Figure 6.1 The structure of fantasy

As we can see in this diagram, the subject is faced with the abyss of the desire of the Other: what does the Other want from me? In order to 'satisfy' this desire and conceal the abyss, the subject responds with a fantasy. The fantasy therefore realizes the desire of the Other. I am not sure what the Other wants, but they seem to like me eating strawberry cake so I will therefore eat strawberry cake in order to try to satisfy their desire. In terms of racism, the intersubjective element of fantasy means that, paradoxically, the racist stages the desire of his victim. The racist, confronted with the abyss of the Jew's desire, makes sense of it by constructing a fantasy in which the Jew is at the centre of some nefarious plot, such as to take over the world. In this way, the desire of the racist to rid the country of Jews is actually a means of concealing the anxiety generated by the desire of the Jews.

LOOKING THROUGH THE FANTASY WINDOW

Žižek often conceives of fantasy as a kind of frame through which we see reality. This frame offers a particular or subjective view of reality. It is permeated with desire and desire is always 'interested', that is, it always presupposes a certain point of view. What Žižek means by this can be understood by reference to the concept of an anamorphosis. An anamorphosis is an image distorted in such a way that it is only recognizable from a specific angle. It is, as Žižek states, 'the element that, when viewed straightforwardly, remains a meaningless stain, but which, as soon as we look at the picture from a precisely determined lateral perspective, all of a sudden acquires well-known contours' (*LA*: 91). The most often-cited example of anamorphosis is a picture entitled *The Ambassadors* by the German painter Hans Holbein (1497–1543). Ostensibly this is just a portrait of two foreign emissaries, then at the court of Henry VIII, showing them amid all the accoutrements of Renaissance learning. However, at the bottom of the picture is an elongated stain which, when viewed from the side, reveals itself to be a skull. This anamorphic reminder of death alters the meaning of the picture, staining all the worldly accomplishments it depicts with a sense of futility and vanity. It is not part of the field of the rest of the painting yet, at the same time, it utterly changes the meaning of the rest of the painting. In the same way, ' "fantasy" designates an element which "sticks out", which cannot be integrated into the given symbolic structure, yet which, precisely as such, constitutes its identity' (*EYS*: 89).

We may think of this element that 'sticks out' as a surplus knowledge, one that contaminates the gaze, subjectivizing the viewer and making it impossible to look at the picture in an objective or neutral fashion. In fact, it is possible to be more precise here and say that an anamorphosis is only the materialization of a surplus knowledge. The stain of the skull in *The Ambassadors*, for example, merely gives body to the knowledge that death is always the conclusion awaiting humankind however clever we may be. Anamorphosis is, therefore, a form of suspense – it suspends the ostensive meaning of a picture or situation. If, for example, we look at a piece of film which shows someone in a house idly making some dinner while listening to phone messages, this seems like an innocuous, mundane shot. If, however, previous to this shot, we see the same house from the outside with someone creeping about in the bushes, wearing a mask and wielding a knife, this completely changes the meaning of the second shot. The first shot stains the second one. We now have a surplus knowledge which contaminates our gaze. There is no stain on the screen in front of us, but everything the person in the house does in the second shot is denatured by the knowledge we have that that person is under threat from the stalker outside.

Ultimately, what anamorphosis represents is subjectivity itself. For subjectivity is precisely such a surplus knowledge. It is that which cannot remain neutral or objective but which looks at the world awry or from a particular point of view. Racism is exemplary in this regard. Shortly after the beginning of the allied bombing of Afghanistan in 2001, the American President George W. Bush (b. 1946) made an address to the American nation on television where he quoted from a letter written to him by the daughter of a military person engaged in the conflict. The letter stated that as much as the girl did not want her father to fight, she was willing to give him up for the war. For President Bush, this was a supreme example of American patriotism. Žižek suggests that we perform a simple mental experiment with regard to this event and imagine the same letter being written by an eight-year-old Afghan girl. Would we (in the West) not denounce this action as the work of a cynical, manipulating fundamentalist? Žižek supposes we would. The difference between interpreting the letter as the product of patriotism or as the product of manipulation is the surplus knowledge informing our perceptions. If we are American subjects, our gaze is stained by American history, customs and traditions. Our interpretation of the Afghan letter is anamorphically distorted by the 'knowledge' we have of Afghanistan as the centre of fundamentalism, as the enemy of our country, and so on. How we apprehend the ethnic 'other' is always subject to the ethnic stain of our own origins.

An anamorphosis, then, is a point of view – it frames reality. In this sense it is analogous to fantasy which is a kind of anamorphic frame around reality. Nowhere is this more clearly realized than in Hitchcock's film, and one of Žižek's favourite references, *Rear Window*. Stuck in a wheelchair because of a broken leg, L.B. 'Jeff' Jeffries, played by James Stewart, is forced to contemplate life through a window, observing people in the other apartments across the yard. Stewart's neutral gaze is subjectivized when he glimpses a murder and catches the eye of the murderer himself. Stewart becomes obsessed with the murderer and is forced to confront the question of '*Che vuoi?*' – what does he actually want from the murder? Why is the murderer the object of his desire? The answer to this question, according to Žižek, is that the murderer stages Stewart's desire. Stewart's desire is centred upon avoiding a sexual relationship with Lisa Carol Fremont, played by Grace Kelly, who constantly attends him in his apartment. The window through which Stewart observes the occupants of the other flats is thus a fantasy frame. Through it he sees what could happen to him and Kelly – they could become like the newlyweds, he could abandon her so she would end up like the lonely artist, and so on. Or, ultimately, he could do away with the problem of Kelly altogether and kill her like the murderer kills his wife. Stewart's attitude towards the murderer is thus predicated upon the surplus knowledge or anamorphic stain of his relationship with Kelly. His point of view is skewed or framed by the interest of his desire in a way that is embodied by the fantasy screen of the window.

Stewart's response to the murder is, therefore, particular to him – it is framed by his own specific fantasy. He does not witness the slaying of his neighbour from an impartial point of view. Indeed, Žižek makes it clear that without our own specific fantasies we would be left not with a sober, objective version of reality, but with no access to reality at all:

> With regard to the basic opposition between reality and imagination, fantasy is not simply on the side of imagination; fantasy is, rather, the little piece of imagination by which we gain access to reality – the frame that guarantees our access to reality, our 'sense of reality' (when our fundamental fantasy is shattered, we experience the 'loss of reality').
>
> (*TZR*: 122)

Despite its everyday connotations, then, fantasy is not just a flight of fancy or an imaginative indulgence. On the contrary, it is the vista from which we see the world. It is the slant with which we are enabled to look at reality.

Furthermore, for Žižek, the slant or point of view of our most fundamental fantasy is what objectively makes us subjective. Our roles in the Symbolic Order can be filled by anyone. You may well be the best baker in town and think yourself indispensable as such. However, should you disappear, another baker will knead your dough, bake your bread and ice your cakes and thereby essentially fill your role. Nevertheless, what is indispensable about you, what remains objectively unique about you is your fantasy. So even when it becomes possible to duplicate your exact genetic make-up down to the last of the six billion elements of code which comprise your objective body, you will still not be cloned because the fantasmatic core which makes you an individual is not reproducible. There may well be other bakers, but there will never be another you.

In order to illustrate the particularity of fantasy, Žižek often has recourse to the novel *Nineteen Eighty-Four* by English writer George Orwell (1903–1950), and specifically the reading of it given by the American philosopher Richard Rorty (b. 1931). As is well known, the culmination of the torture of Winston, the novel's leading character, is reached in Room 101, the place where a victim's worst fears are realized. Up to this point, Winston has betrayed everyone and everything he believes in except his love for Julia. However, here, with a cage containing rats attached to his face, Winston utterly breaks down, betraying Julia completely:

> 'Do it to Julia! Do it to Julia! Not me! Julia! I don't care what you do to her. Tear her face off, strip her to the bones. Not me! Julia! Not me!'
>
> He was falling backwards, into enormous depths, away from the rats. He was still strapped in the chair, but he had fallen through the floor, through the walls of the building, through the earth, through the oceans, through the atmosphere, into outer space, into the gulfs between the stars.
>
> (Orwell 1949: 300)

What Winston betrays here is not just Julia but himself, the specificity of his being as it is contained in his fundamental fantasy. The 'Do it to Julia!' is, according to Rorty, 'the sentence he could not utter sincerely and still be able to put himself back together' (Rorty 1989: 179). Žižek concurs with this analysis but argues that where Rorty identifies this as a breakdown in the Symbolic (because it is a sentence or signifying formation), Žižek proposes that what Winston forgoes here is actually his fundamental fantasy, that which 'sticks out' from the Symbolic. This fantasy is the support of his being and without it he falls into the abyss, 'into the gulf between the stars'. Winston's universe collapses because he no longer has the specificity of his own view, his own fantasy frame. He thus spends the remainder of the novel as an unthinking being, an automaton who is merely part of the Big Brother machine.

As each individual's fantasy is the support of his or her being, it is little wonder that it is, Žižek avows, extremely precious and therefore sensitive to the encroachment of others. Fantasy is, as it were, the tender nerve or raw ganglia of the subject's psyche, and it is liable to cause grave distress if we probe it with insufficient care. As an example of this, Žižek discusses 'Black House', a short story by the American author, and perennial Žižekian favourite, Patricia Highsmith (1921–1995). The story follows a young man who has just moved into a small American town. In the saloon he listens to the local men recount tales from their youth of their adventures in and around the black house on the hill. This house is a desolate building which, they claim, is either haunted or inhabited by a homicidal maniac or, in some other way, malevolent. Determined to verify this, the young man goes to the house the next evening and finds nothing but an old ruin devoid of any threat, supernatural or otherwise. When he returns to the saloon to inform the men of his findings they are horrified. One of them then attacks the man, an act which ultimately results in the young man's death. The reason for this behaviour, according to Žižek, is that the black house functioned as a fantasy screen upon which the men could project their nostalgic desires. By empirically proving that the house was just an old ruin, the young man inadvertently intruded upon that fantasy space. Where the young man saw just a decaying building, the men in the saloon saw it from the particular perspective of their fantasy and therefore imbued it with a meaning he could not fathom. The violent reaction of the men is thus caused by the young man annulling 'the difference between reality and fantasy space, depriving the men of the place in which they were able to articulate their desires' (*LA*: 9).

THE ETHNIC FANTASY

With this discussion of fantasy, we may appear to have drifted away from the topic of racism, but Žižek's contention is that what is at stake in so-called 'ethnic tension' is a conflict of fantasies. The standard analysis of racism contends that racists are misguided, uneducated or in some way ignorant of those they victimize. If only, so the theory goes, the racist could see them objectively, get to know them, his or

POSTMODERN RACISM

Žižek contends that today racism is just as reflexive as every other part of postmodern life. It is not the product of ignorance in the way it used to be. So, whereas racism used to involve a claim that another ethnic group is inherently inferior to our own, racism is now articulated in terms of a respect for another's culture. If racists once said, 'My culture is better than yours', postmodern or reflexive racism centres around the assertion that, 'My culture is different from yours'. As an example of this Žižek asks 'was not the official argument for apartheid in the old South Africa that black culture should be preserved in its uniqueness, not dissipated in the Western melting-pot?' (*TFA*: 6). What is at stake here, according to Žižek, is the fetishistic disavowal of cynicism: 'I know very well that all ethnic cultures are equal in value, yet, nevertheless, I will act as if mine is superior'. The split evident here between the subject of enunciated (the 'I know very well . . .') and the subject of the enunciation (the 'nevertheless I act as if I didn't') is even preserved when racists are asked to explain the reasons for their racist behaviour. Typically, a racist will blame his or her socio-economic environment, poor childhood, peer group pressure, and so on, in such a way as to suggest to Žižek that he or she cannot help being racist, but is merely a victim of circumstances. Thus postmodern racists are fully able to rationalize their behaviour in a way that belies the traditional image of racism as the vocation of the ignorant.

her prejudices would melt away. If, for example, the German racist could only see what a huge economic contribution the Turkish immigrants make to the German economy. If only the French racists could see what important cultural achievements the Algerian community has made in the name of France. If only the British racists could understand the vital contributions of second and third generation Indians to the health of the United Kingdom. And if only they could, according to Žižek, they would *still* be racists. Why?

The answer to this question is that the subject of racism is not an objective collection of individuals but a fantasy figure. In the 1930s, for example, the Nazis could not have been persuaded by rational argumentation that the Jews were not really at the centre of some international plot to undermine the Aryan race. You could not, argues Žižek, present them with empirical evidence proving that the Jews were really not like that because, like the men in the saloon talking about the black house, they were not dealing with an objective view of reality. Rather, they were looking at the Jews from the point of view of a fantasy frame. You could not, then, contrast that fantasy frame with a view of reality because the whole point of a fantasy frame is that it constitutes your reality in the first place. So even if, as Žižek conjectures, you were a Nazi who lived next door to a real, neighbourly 'good' Jew, you would not experience any contradiction between your anti-Semitism and this neighbour. You would, rather, conclude that your neighbour proves quite how dangerous Jews are because they seem such decent people on the surface. The very facts which would seem to contradict your anti-Semitism would actually prove to be arguments in its favour precisely because you saw those facts through your fantasy window.

All of which begs the question: what is the racist fantasy? For Žižek, there are two basic racist fantasies. The first type of racist fantasy centres around the apprehension that the ethnic 'other' desires our enjoyment. 'They' want to steal our enjoyment from 'us' and rob us of the specificity of our fantasy. The second type of racist fantasy proceeds from an uneasiness that the ethnic 'other' has access to some strange *jouissance*. 'They' do not do things like 'us'. The way 'they' enjoy themselves is alien and unfamiliar. What both these fantasies are predicated upon, then, is that the 'other' enjoys in a different way to 'us':

> In short, what really gets on our nerves, what really bothers us about the 'other', is the peculiar way he organizes his enjoyment (the smell of his food, his 'noisy' songs and dances, his strange manners, his attitude to work – in the racist perspective, the 'other' is either a workaholic stealing our jobs or an idler living on our labour).

> (*LA*: 165)

In other words, ethnic tension is caused by a conflict of fantasies, if, in this regard, we understand fantasy as a way of organizing enjoyment. The specificity of *their* fantasy conflicts with the specificity of *our* fantasy. So, for example, a strand of American racism is 'bothered' by the way the Japanese seem to enjoy working and work at enjoyment. The Japanese, by American conventions, do not know how to separate work from play – their relationship to enjoyment is in some way disturbed or 'not normal'. They are therefore a 'threat' to the American way of life.

For Žižek, this 'threat', or at least the perception of a threat, is a growing one. The past couple of decades have witnessed a marked rise in racial tension and ethnic nationalism. Žižek, following Lacan and Marx, ascribes this rise to the process of globalization. 'Globalization' refers to the way in which capitalism has spread across the world, displacing indigenous companies in favour of multinational businesses. The effects of this process are not necessarily just commercial, for what is at stake here are the national cultures and political bodies which underpin, and are supported by, resident industries. When a multi-national business like McDonald's opens up in Bombay, for example, it is not just another business, but represents a specifically American approach to food, culture and, ultimately, social organization. The more capitalism spreads, the more it works to dissolve the efficacy of national domains, dissipating local traditions and values in favour of universal ones.

The only way to offset this increased homogeneity and to assert the worth of the particular against the global is to cling with ever greater tenacity to your specific ethnic fantasy, the point of view which makes you Indian, British or German. And if you are busy trying to avoid being dissolved in the multicultural mix of globalization by sticking to the way you organize your enjoyment, you will inevitably court the risk of succumbing to a racist paranoia. Even if we attempt to insti-tute a form of equality between the ways in which we organize our enjoyment, unfortunately, as Žižek points out, 'fantasies cannot coexist peacefully' (*LA*: 168). One of the most common examples of this problem is so-called arranged marriages. If a couple's enjoyment is organized around the formal process of selection, restricted meetings and so on which culminate in an arranged marriage, as it is in some cultures, are we, who consider such arrangements to be the very antithesis of free, spontaneous love, not then imposing our own fantasies on the couple if we step in and stop these marriages taking place? Is this part of their 'right to enjoyment', or are we supposed to liberate them in the name of Western values from this archaic way of organizing their enjoyment? The answer, for Žižek, is that there is no way to establish a compromise between the two fantasies at stake here.

THE ETHICS OF FANTASY

How, then, are we to proceed? What is the way of avoiding a clash of ethnic fantasies? Žižek's first answer to this is to propose a kind of ethics of fantasy. Simply stated, this proposes that we try as much as possible not to violate the fantasy space of the 'other', the specific way in which an individual looks at the world. This does not mean that we love our neighbour in so far as he or she resembles ourselves, nor that we love our neighbour because of his or her Symbolic mandate, even if we stretch that mandate to include his or her status as a human being. In other words, we do not respect 'others' for any universal feature that they might share with us, but rather for what they do not share with us, which is their fantasy. We therefore do our utmost *not* to prove that what they think is a house full of significant meaning is actually a ruined old shack as the young man does in Patricia Highsmith's 'Black House'.

Of course, as fantasies cannot ultimately coexist peacefully, particularly when they are ethnic fantasies, this ethic can only ever be an intermediate solution. For the present, Žižek has a more practical solution to the problem of racism, one which draws on his own experience in Slovenia. Surprisingly for a revolutionary, Žižek argues that we should support the state in opposition to civil society. By 'state' Žižek here means to refer to the institutions of government, whereas 'civil society' designates, in its widest sense, the people of a nation or non-governmental groups. While Žižek might aspire to a nation based purely on the consensual will of civil society, he contends that, in the light of the currently existing racist fantasies of much of civil society, this is just not possible. If he finds this in Slovenia, where he argues that civil society is basically right-wing, Žižek also sees it, for example, in the United States:

> In America, after the Oklahoma bombing, they suddenly discovered that there are hundreds of thousands of jerks. Civil society is not this nice, social movement, but a network of moral majority conservatives and nationalist pressure groups, against abortion, for religious education in schools. A real pressure from below.
>
> (Lovink 1995)

Žižek's argument is that the state can act as a buffer between the fantasies of different groups, mitigating the worst effects of those fantasies. If civil society were allowed to rule unrestrained, much of the world would succumb to racist violence. It is only the forces of the state which keep it in check.

In the long term, Žižek argues that in order to avoid a clash of fantasies we have to learn to 'traverse the fantasy'. What Žižek means by this is that we have to acknowledge that fantasy merely functions to screen the abyss or inconsistency in the Other which we noted earlier. In 'traversing' or 'going through' the fantasy, then, 'all we have to do,' according to Žižek, 'is experience how there is nothing "behind" it, and how fantasy masks precisely this "nothing"' (*SOI*: 126). But how does this apply to racism?

The subject of racism, be it the Jew, the Turk, the Algerian, or whoever, is a fantasy figure, someone who embodies the void of the Other. The underlying argument of all racism is that 'if only *they* weren't here, life would be perfect, and society would be harmonious again'. However, as Žižek points out, what this argument misses is the fact that because the subject of racism is only a fantasy figure, it is only there to make us think that such a harmonious society is actually possible in the first place. In actuality, according to Žižek, society is always-already divided. The fantasy racist figure is just a way of covering up the impossibility of a whole society or an organic Symbolic Order complete unto itself:

> What appears as the hindrance to society's full identity with itself is actually its positive condition: by transposing onto the Jew the role of the foreign body which introduces in the social organism disintegration and antagonism, the fantasy-image of society *qua* consistent, harmonious whole is rendered possible.
>
> (*EYS*: 90)

Which is another way of saying that if the Jew qua (or 'in his or her status or role as a') fantasy figure, was not there, we would have to invent it in order to maintain the illusion that we could have a perfect society. For all the fantasy racist figure does is embody the existing impossibility of a harmonious or complete society.

If, as Žižek suggests, we learn to traverse the fantasy, we will come to recognize that the characteristics attributed to the fantasy figure of racism are 'nothing' more than the products of our own system. Instead of saying 'if only *they* weren't here, life would be perfect, and society would be harmonious again', we will say 'whether they are here or not, society is always-already divided'. By traversing the fantasy in this way we will accept that the figures of racism embody the truth of the failure of our society to constitute itself as complete. Instead of vilifying other cultures, therefore, Žižek enjoins us to come together in the '"solidarity of a common struggle", when [we] discover that the deadlock which hampers [us] is also the deadlock which hampers the Other' (*TTS*: 220). What kind of a society this 'common struggle' might lead to, Žižek, like everyone else, is unsure, but he remains hopeful.

SUMMARY

For Žižek, racism is produced by a clash of fantasies rather than by a clash of symbols vying for supremacy. There are several distinguishing features of fantasy:

1   Fantasies are produced as a defence against the desire of the Other manifest in the '*Che vuoi?*', the question of what the Other, in its inconsistency, really wants from me.
2   Fantasies provide a framework through which we see reality. They are anamorphic in that they presuppose a point of view, denying us an objective account of the world.
3   Fantasies are the one unique thing about us. They are what make us individuals, allowing a subjective view of reality. As such, our fantasies are extremely sensitive to the intrusion of others.
4   Fantasies are the way in which we organize and domesticate our enjoyment or *jouissance*.

There are two basic racist fantasies:

1   The ethnic 'other' has a strange or privileged access to *jouissance*.
2   The ethnic 'other' is trying to steal our *jouissance*.

In each case, what is at stake is an attempt to maintain the particularity of the racist's fantasy, his or her way of organizing enjoyment, in the face of a globalization which threatens to swamp that particularity within a universal. As fantasy is immune to rational argument, Žižek suggests that we can only combat racism by proceeding on three fronts. First, we must try not to intrude on the fantasy space of other individuals wherever possible. Second, Žižek proposes that we continue to use the state as a buffer against the fantasies of civil society. Third, he advocates the practice of traversing or going through the fantasy, to show that, on the other side of fantasy, there is nothing there.

AFTER ŽIŽEK

THE CURSE OF JACQUES: LIMITATIONS ON THE INFLUENCE OF ŽIŽEK

Žižek is a relative newcomer to the English-speaking world of critical theory. Although he has produced a substantial body of work (25 books and counting), it has largely been published within the space of a decade. As academia habitually operates at a rather more leisurely pace than Žižek, it has not yet had time to come to terms with the astonishing output of what one critic has described as 'one of the great minds of our time' (*TARS*: viii). Indeed, what is striking about Žižek is that he has had quite the impact that he has in such a short duration. This is all the more impressive given that what has been essential to this impact is also the very feature of Žižek's work which undoubtedly impedes its appeal: his Lacanianism.

The perspicacity of Žižek's insights relies heavily upon the Lacanian paradigm and its synaesthetic infusion with Hegel and Marx. Unfortunately, as if being an adherent of Hegel and Marx is not awkward enough in a post-structuralist dominated era, his advocacy of Lacan is more or less downright embarrassing. This might seem a strange assertion, but the difficulty of Žižek's Lacanian position proceeds from two points. First, according to Žižek, the field of theory is structured around the exclusion of Lacan – one is tempted to say that Lacan is the *sinthome* of academic theory – he is the surplus that binds the otherwise disparate groupings of theorists together. Deconstructionists do not like him, the followers of Foucault do not like him, the feminists do not like him – nobody likes him, and despite their many internal differences, all these other theoretical groupings agree on this one point. The life of a self-proclaimed Lacanian, such as Žižek, can therefore be a difficult one, as he points out:

> Let's not forget that academia is itself an 'Ideological State Apparatus', and that all these orientations are not simply theoretical orientations, but what's in question is thousands of posts, departmental politics, and so on. Lacanians are excluded from this. That is to say, we are not a field. You know, Derrida has his own empire, Habermasians have their own empire – dozens of departments, all connected – but with Lacanians, it's not like this. It's maybe a person here, a person there, usually marginal positions.
>
> (Hanlon 2001: 12–13)

Jacques Derrida and Jacques Lacan famously had a disagreement in the 1970s and there has been a certain degree of tension between their adherents ever since. As Derrideans, Habermasians, and other groupings tend to hold the majority hand in theoretically oriented departments, Lacanians have, in Žižek's eyes, been somewhat marginalized. While some may argue that Žižek is wrong on this point, the setbacks that Žižek suffered at the beginning of his career, in part due to his deployment of Lacan's theories, have perhaps left him more politically sensitive in this regard.

The second, and related, point is that the work of Lacan, upon which Žižek repeatedly draws, is not only extremely difficult in itself, but it is also very difficult to get hold of. The publishing history of Lacan's work is mired in controversy, but much of it is only available to the Lacanian elite centred around Lacan's son-in-law. That which is available very often only attests to some of Lacan's earlier theories – the very ones that Žižek decries throughout his work. De facto, therefore, Žižek himself functions as a substitute Lacan for much of the English-speaking world. Žižek's interpretations of Lacan are thus, in large measure, for the majority of his readers, the theories of Lacan themselves. If Lacan is the *sinthome* of academic theory, 'Žižek' is the name we call it.

One advantage that Žižek has been able to secure from this seemingly onerous position is that of being able to establish *his* version of Lacan. The Lacan you have read about in these pages is, in large part,

Žižek's own. Before Žižek, much of the work inspired by Lacanian psychoanalysis featured the Imaginary and, in some cases, the Symbolic. After Žižek, however, our attention has been redirected to the interplay of these two Orders with that of the Real. This is crucial because it radically alters the status of the subject. No longer is the subject a post-structuralist cliché left to the mercy of signifiers, one for whom they bob autonomously up and down in some kind of sub-Derridean merry-go-round. Nor do we have to return to a thoroughly metaphysical subject, busily assuming mastery over an obedient universe while somehow remaining immune to the forces exerted by that universe. Rather, the interplay between the Real and the Symbolic and Imaginary Orders allows for a subject which is constructed both in and beyond language and is therefore both a captive of the Symbolic and independent of it. Žižek has returned a degree of subtlety to our conception of the subject: we are both in and out of ideology, condemned to gender but able to change it, fixed in our ethnic fantasies yet able to traverse them. We are, as it were, part of the system but more than it at the same time.

Žižek's understanding of the Real is inextricably linked with his ingenious reading of Hegel. Again, the Hegel you have been reading about in this book is very much Žižek's Hegel – (if you are in any doubt about this, read Žižek's recent collaboration with Ernesto Laclau and Judith Butler, *Contingency, Hegemony, Universality*, which partly discusses the legacy of Hegel). For most critics, Hegel is the philosopher of dialectical synthesis, an arch metaphysician of totalitarian logic for whom the whole is prized above the parts that make up that whole. As such, he is rather anachronistic in an era where we value the particular and decry even the possibility of achieving the universal except, as is often claimed, at the expense of disregarding the merits of the specific. While Žižek abhors the theoretical confusion between the totality (the conception of the whole) and totalitarianism (the unmitigated rule of the whole) which usually underpins such claims, his Hegel is far more subtle than he is conventionally depicted.

In particular, Žižek has developed Hegel's notion of 'concrete universality'. This notion is essentially summed up in the phrase 'the genus that is always one of its own species' which I mentioned in Chapter 5. What this means for Žižek is that the assertion of a particular position necessarily entails the assertion of a universal position. For example, if we look at religion, what we are normally tempted to say is that there is the universal concept or genus of religion, and that within that there are particular varieties or species of religion, such as Christianity, Judaism, Islam, and so on. However, Žižek argues that each species of religion presupposes a general definition of religion as a genus or universal concept:

> Christianity is not simply different from Judaism and Islam; within its horizon, the very difference that separates it from the other two 'religions of the Book' appears in a way which is unacceptable for the other two. In other words, when a Christian debates with a Muslim, they do not simply disagree – they disagree about their very disagreement: about what makes the difference between their religions.
>
> (*CHU*: 315)

Žižek makes a similar point about the difference between the political left and right. It is not just that they disagree about this or that particular point but about the whole terrain of politics. This is why he argues the idea of a 'middle ground' or 'Third Way', which has been advocated by the leaders of the political left such as Tony Blair and Bill Clinton, actually marks the death-knell of politics. The 'Third Way' is an acceptance by the left of the first principle of the right, i.e. of the necessity of capitalism. It is not a neutral form of politics, mediating between left and right; it is, for Žižek, simply a right-wing politics.

Reading politics via Hegel's notion of concrete universality means that each particular stance supposes its own universal form of politics and that, following from this, there cannot be an impartial, middle-of-the-road way to arbitrate between them. Equally, at a philosophical level, Žižek's Hegel is not, as his critics suggest, the advocate of a totalitarian logic. This is because the totality, for Žižek's Hegel, is always fissured or split within itself. Each particularity or part of the totality reconfigures the universal, transforming the very character of the totality:

> The paradox of the proper Hegelian notion of the Universal is that it is not the neutral frame of the multitude of particular contents, but inherently divisive, splitting up its particular content: the Universal always asserts itself in the guise of some particular content which claims to embody it directly, excluding all other content as merely particular.
>
> (*TTS*: 101)

The totality is, therefore, never without remainder. There is always an element that 'sticks out'; the particular that determines the universal yet is also part of it. So, with religion, Christianity is the element that sticks out if you are a Christian, whereas Islam is the element that sticks out of the totality of religion if you are a Muslim.

This reading of Hegel, which for many critics has nothing whatsoever to do with Hegel, is one of Žižek's great achievements as a thinker. It is centred, as was noted earlier, around an oxymoronic style of thought. This style of thought is one which Žižek applies to all his subject matter. Most notable in this regard is the matter of the subject itself which, he argues, constitutes itself only in so far as it is alien to itself. The truth of the subject is always outside itself in the object. It is the element that sticks out of the universal. With this one point, Žižek radically alters the centuries-old conception of the subject and the object as mutually opposed terms. In so doing, he makes a telling contribution to some of the most pressing problems facing critical thought today.

For example, one of the most fiercely debated questions in recent years has been whether or not we are stuck in the present, unable to know the past because all we can do is reinterpret it according to our own values. Reviewed in the light of Žižek's reading of Hegel, however, we can see how it is actually impossible fully to subjectivize the past precisely because our own subjectivity is incomplete. Our subjectivity is predicated upon a relationship with the objective world which means that it cannot 'overwhelm' the object or fully subjectivize it. Equally, those who argue that the subject is at the mercy of objective historical forces, that, in other words, the object 'overwhelms' the subject, miss the fact the relationship also works the other way. The object is dependent for its status as an object on there being a subject to differentiate it as such. Which is to say that the object of the past is as liable to the identity of the subject as the subject is to the identity of the object of the past. The object of the past invades the subject of the present, just as much as the subject of the present overwhelms the object of the past. There is, in other words, no pure subjectivity any more than there is any pure objectivity.

This approach, it seems to me, has many points of convergence with Derrida's writing on history. Indeed, Derrida's whole oeuvre could be characterized as a commentary on the non-identity of time with itself. For Derrida the experience of the subject is never synchronous with itself; it is always self-divided or split. Nowhere is this more evident than in his theory of language – language being the way in which the subject represents its experience to itself. Like Lacan, Derrida bases his theory of language on the work of Saussure. Derrida argues that sense, or the meaning of a signifier, is always deferred. We can never know what one signifier means without making reference to another signifier. The totality of a signifier, we might say, is therefore never without remainder – the remainder of another signifier. In this way, no one signifier can find its identity with itself because a signifier is never a complete entity. Another signifier always 'sticks out' of the whole of the original signifier, conferring meaning upon it, ad infinitum.

If Derrida's work can then be characterized as an extended analysis of the non-identity of time with itself, it is equally possible to characterize Žižek's whole oeuvre as a commentary on the lack of identity with itself. They are both dealing with a lack of balance, a constitutive 'out-of-jointness' of the totality. For each of them, there is always an element of the whole that 'sticks out' and mars the integrity of that whole. At his most critical, however, and perhaps in keeping with this characterization of his philosophy, Žižek disavows the possibility of any *rapprochement* between Derridean deconstruction and Lacanian psychoanalysis, claiming that 'all attempts to mediate between them ultimately fall short' (Hanlon 2001: 13). In his more optimistic analyses of the two schools of thought, however, he declares that if 'we set aside major confrontations and tackle the problematic nature of their relationship *en détail*, as befits Freudians, a series of unexpected connections opens up' (*TMOE*: 193). There are some critics, most notably Laclau, who concur with this latter assertion. Laclau has attempted to put Derridean deconstruction and a Žižek-inspired Lacanian psychoanalysis into productive tension within the framework of a political ('post-Marxist') analysis of society. The fascinating results of this collaboration hopefully anticipate a time when the theory community is no longer divided by the name of 'Jacques' and Žižek's work will therefore be able to find a wider constituency than at present.

LEFTISM

If Žižek's reading of Hegel has changed our understanding of the dialectic, the way in which the parts interact with the whole, it has done so as part of a larger project for Žižek – that of reactualizing the whole tradition of German Idealism. Žižek has helped to return Kant and the oft-neglected Schelling to the forefront of critical theory. In part, this is of a piece with a trend in recent years for critical theory to re-examine its roots, both in order to appoint lines of succession and to find in its heritage connections between various different orientations. Žižek's most notable achievement in this area has been to establish the ways in which idealism laid the groundwork for materialism and the theories of Marx. Indeed, he has even found in Christianity, seemingly one of the great avatars of idealism, a model for Marxist political revolution. And this – the hope of a political revolution – is where Žižek's ideas ultimately always orient themselves. Although he clearly delights in ideas for their own sake, there is always a purpose informing his play – Marxism.

Given the relatively brief lives of both disciplines, there has been a long tradition of collaboration between psychoanalysis and Marxism. This tradition stretches back to the late 1920s, when the Austrian-American psychoanalyst and 'cloudbuster' Wilhelm Reich (1897–1957) deployed an awkward synthesis of Freud and Marx in order to analyse political behaviours, and it reached its zenith of popularity during the1960s in the now-neglected work of the German-American philosopher and social activist Herbert Marcuse (1898–1979). Žižek's fusion of Marx and Lacan, however, represents, along with the work of Fredric Jameson, by far the most sophisticated welding of the two theories to date. Whereas, for Jameson, previous amalgamations of Marxism and psychoanalysis 'now seem dated' (Jameson 1988a: 80), Žižek's contribution to the canon seems more likely to endure because it takes both disciplines seriously and does not use either one as a 'bolt-on extra'.

Žižek has also advanced our understanding of the methodological similarities between Marxism and psychoanalysis. As Žižek avers, at the foundation of both disciplines is an attempt to formulate theories which will help to change the material world: Marxism aims to improve society, and psychoanalysis aims to improve its patients. In other words, both disciplines are not, as Žižek points out, simply theories of their respective objects (society and the unconscious) in the way that physics is a study of its object; rather, Marxism and psychoanalysis are attempts to transform the objects of their study. There is always a practical intent underlying both disciplines, and while Žižek is not particularly interested in helping patients, he has done more than any other theorist to disinter the political Lacan and to put his ideas into the service of a revolutionary politics.

In this regard, Žižek's most telling contributions to Marxism have been to furnish it with an adequate model of the subject and to relate that model to traditional Marxist concepts, such as ideology, history and the totality. Žižek's reading of Lacanian psychoanalysis is particularly valuable here because it is not really a psychology, in the sense of dealing with people's inner thoughts and feelings, but rather a theory for which the unconscious is always outside, materialized in rituals and practices. In other words, Žižek's psychoanalysis sets out in step with Marxism, identifying the social as the most efficacious field for analysis because it mediates between the political and the individual.

Žižek has also used Hegelian philosophy to reinvigorate contemporary Marxism. Initially, this might well sound like a retrograde step, given that Marx famously 'stood Hegel on his head', substituting Hegel's idealism with his own materialist theories. However, Žižek's use of Hegel is set against the conception of politics advanced by the French sociologist Michel Foucault (1926–1984) which is currently that favoured by most theorists on the left. According to Žižek, Foucault proposes that state power is an agent of constraint, controlling who should be included and who should be excluded from society. In this model, state power is exercised from the centre of society. Resistance to that power, on the other hand, is vainly perpetrated from the margins of society by those who lack a proper Symbolic identity. The struggle for power is thus conceived as a battle which involves the agents of the margins resisting the power of a centralized state. The irony here, however, is that Foucault argues all such marginal resistance is actually generated by the centre of Power itself and is therefore co-opted in advance.

What such a model of politics forgets, for Žižek, is that state power is itself split. Far from being universal or homogeneous entities, the apparatuses of state are, Žižek argues, 'supplemented by their shadowy double, by a network of publicly disavowed rituals, unwritten rules, institutions, practices, and so on' (*CHU*: 313). In other words, that which is 'officially' marginalized by state power is already constitutive of it, supporting it in the shadowy underside of politics. Žižek finds an example of this in *A Few Good Men*, the film which follows the trial of two American soldiers accused of murdering a fellow soldier.

The central issue of the trial concerns the existence or not of the so-called 'Code Red'. A 'Code Red' is essentially an authorized act of transgression in which a superior officer condones the illegal punishment of a soldier for breaking the 'ethical' conventions of the unit. What Žižek finds interesting about this 'Code Red' is that it must remain unacknowledged. Officially it does not exist because it violates the written law, yet, at the same time, submission to this unwritten law is the surest way to assert membership of the community of soldiers.

For Žižek, this is emblematic of all power structures. On one side there is the public written law, the rule of the Symbolic, and on the other side is what he terms the obscene law of the superego, the unwritten law which, by its transgressive character, supports the meaning of the law with enjoyment:

> Such a code must remain under cover of night, unacknowledged, unutterable – in public, everybody pretends to know nothing about it, or even actively denies its existence. It represents the 'spirit of community' at its purest, exerting the strongest pressure on the individual to comply with its mandate of group identification. Yet, simultaneously, it violates the explicit rules of community life.
>
> (*TMOE*: 54)

This analysis of power is Hegelian for Žižek in so far as it identifies the exception to the universal as the linchpin of the universal. In this case, then, it is the act of transgression which supports the law it is transgressing. Unlike the Foucaldian model of power as a homogeneous totality incorporating resistance within it, Žižek's Hegelian-inspired conception of the totality of power finds that it is always disturbed by an excess which it can never quite control. If this is so, how then, should marginalized groups tackle the inequitable application of power?

One solution is for societies to minister explicitly to marginalized groups. Most Western states now attempt to do this with race, gender and other group-specific legislation. However, as Žižek suggests, such an approach inevitably courts the frustrations of those to whom it ministers precisely because it is so group-specific. The very specificity of a legislation addressed to exact predicaments bars the possibility of the wrong it addresses being elevated to a universal complaint.

The subjects of the legislation thus feel access to the Symbolic whole is denied them. Instead of this, one of the ways forward, for Žižek, is to exploit the split in the apparatuses of power between the written and unwritten law which sustains it. In this sense, Žižek finds that the most subversive strategy is actually the one which involves fully submitting to the written law. By keeping rigorously to the law, it is impossible to indulge in the unlawful acts of the superego, those Code Red-like actions which embody the true spirit of the community and thereby support the power of the Symbolic. As an example of such an approach, Žižek points to the work of Czech author Jaroslav Hašek (1883–1923) and particularly *The Good Soldier Schweik*, 'the novel whose hero wreaks total havoc by simply executing the orders of his superiors in an overzealous and all-too-literal way' (*TPOF*: 22).

UNIVERSAL CRITICISM

In view of the sheer amount of work Žižek has published, as well as the range of his topic matter, it is perhaps unsurprising that his ideas have been subject to a certain degree of critique. What is slightly more noteworthy is that most of this criticism has issued from the political left, or what might be considered the natural constituency for an avowed Marxist. However, as I have already noted, the inheritors of the Marxist tradition are not a homogeneous group but, rather, are riven by issues as fundamental as, for example, the workings of ideology, or even the value of Marx's work as a whole. Žižek's unique and substantial interpretation of political philosophy covers many of these issues and he has therefore attracted a number of detractors.

One such critic is the philosopher Peter Dews. In one of the most considered critiques of Žižek's work, Dews systematically dismantles the twin pillars of Žižekian theory: Hegel and Lacan. He argues that Žižek's work is neither properly Hegelian nor properly Lacanian, and that, in misreading both of them, Žižek has arrived at a right-wing politics which only masquerades as a left-wing politics. Dews claims that the results of this confusion can be seen both in Žižek's analysis of modern subjectivity and in his own life:

He views the modern individual as caught in the dichotomy between his or her universal status as a member of civil society, and the particularistic attachments of ethnicity, nation and tradition, and this duality is reflected in his

For a traditional Marxist the word 'nationalistic' is anathema because
it broadly designates 'right-wing'. However, as I noted in the first
chapter of this book, Žižek's support for the non-Marxist liberal party
in Slovenia was actually borne of a desire to prevent the nationalists
from acceding to power by the most expedient means possible, in this
case support for the liberal democratic party. Dews' accusation here
is therefore somewhat misguided. As Žižek remarks, 'in Slovenia,
nationalists cannot stand me' (Hanlon 2001: 7).

If it is unpleasant to be accused of *something*, however misguided the
accusation, it is very much worse to be indicted for *nothing* at all.
Unfortunately for Žižek, this has been a feature of the assessments made
by many of his detractors. For one of the most widely found criticisms
of Žižek is what his critics take to be his inscrutability. Theorists such as
Teresa Ebert and Denise Gigante have censured Žižek for occupy-
ing what they perceive as a transcendental position, one in which he fails
to advance any specific view of his own. His politics are, they claim,
impossible to pin down, as Gigante makes clear:

> Where Žižek is unique, and where he makes his radical break with other literary
> theorists who take up a position, any position at all that pretends to some
> notional content, is the fact that he fundamentally has no position.
>
> (Gigante 1998: 153)

What such criticisms suggest is that Žižek is the very type of cynic he
roundly condemns in his own work. Which is to say that, to put it
bluntly, while he knows that all about him the world is in a terrible
state yet still he fails to advance a way of changing the world. The
theorist Sean Homer is typical when he argues that:

> Žižek's work . . . remains largely within the paradigm of ideology critique, which
> he himself criticises, as he unmasks ideologies such as racism, nationalism
> and anti-Semitism. His work never really moves to that second moment,
> whereby a consideration of what ideology returns to us may facilitate the
> formulation of oppositional ideologies and the space of politics proper. I always
> remain unclear, for example, what Žižek is actually arguing for.
>
> (Homer 1995)

On the one hand, this seems a strange and even galling assertion given not only Žižek's avowed Marxism, but also the personal difficulties he has incurred as the result of his political stand in Slovenia (which, he has pointed out, cost him most of his friends, destroyed his intellectual profile there, and caused him to be incorrectly vilified as a nationalist abroad). On the other hand, we can perhaps understand Homer's point as an exaggerated response to Žižek's insistence on the 'act' as the only authentic way in which to change the world. As an act changes the very horizon of our understanding, it is, by definition, unfeasible for Žižek to specify quite what the world would look like after the advent of an act. He is therefore less concerned to articulate what it is impossible to articulate than he is to maintain the possibility of there being an act at all. As he notes, 'the way the political space is structured today more and more prevents the emergence of the act' (Hanlon 2001: 11). Žižek thus focuses his energies on clearing a place for an act in the political sphere by constantly theorizing the horizon of life under capitalism.

What is interesting about the accusation of inscrutability, particularly from Marxists such as Ebert and Homer, is that it flatly contradicts criticism he has received from feminists who argue that he relegates issues of feminism to a secondary concern behind his critique of capitalism. In other words, they reproach Žižek with being a thorough-going Marxist, one for whom altering the socio-economic organization of the world always ultimately supersedes the need to address the concerns of any specific group – in this case women. This criticism touches upon one of the key issues within the political left for the past thirty years, one which more recently has come to be known as the question of 'identity politics'. Briefly stated, the term 'identity politics', which is a phrase more generally used by its detractors, refers to a politics which acknowledges that specific groups or identities each have their own specific struggles and that, as such, no one group should either be equated with, or privileged over, the other. For example, women, as a group have specific inequalities which they wish to address in a patriarchal society which are not the same as, or more important than, the inequalities which people of a specific ethnic origin wish to address.

While this might seem like an innocuous assertion, it has caused dissent within the ranks of traditional Marxists because it undermines the argument that ultimately, or in the last instance, it is class, or more properly the mode of economic organization which determines inequalities across the planet. In other words, traditional Marxism may very well support the struggles for equality of different groups, but it does so with the proviso that it is ultimately only by changing the current conditions of exploitation under capitalism that things will alter for the better for everybody. For example, if feminists conducted a campaign for equal pay for women in France and they then achieved that, for them it would be the end of the story. For Marxists, however, it would merely mean that somewhere else in the world, the costs of that wage increase for women in France would have to be off-set by the capitalist system by employing child labour at cheaper rates. Which is to say that Marxists claim to look at the total picture of inequality, while, they argue, identity groups only focus on specific grievances, missing how they are all interrelated. Conversely, identity groups aver that Marxists are so preoccupied with the totality of relations they omit to address the specific needs of specific people.

When Žižek is tasked with this argument, his answer is twofold. First, he argues that identity politics is a fully historical phenomenon, but one which ignores its own conditions of possibility. In the case of feminism, why is it, he asks, that a century ago most people were convinced that gender was God-given, but now they are equally convinced that gender is socially constituted?

> It is not that before, people were 'stupid essentialists' and believed in naturalized sexuality, while now they know that genders are performatively enacted; one needs a kind of metanarrative that explains this very passage from essentialism to the awareness of contingency.

(*CHU*: 106)

In other words, Žižek does not think that the emergence of identity politics means that we have suddenly discovered the true facts of the matter about, for example, gender – facts that could have been disclosed a century ago if only people had been clever enough. Rather, Žižek contends that the emergence of identity politics is bound to a specific historical moment. Which is to say that identity politics is part of a larger picture and that we need a metanarrative or totalizing story to explain it. Žižek concedes that such a metanarrative could take many forms, but his preferred version is that of Marxism.

Second, Žižek argues that while identity politics has expanded the terrain of politics into new areas, it has also enfeebled the very notion of the 'political' by doing so:

> Today's postmodern politics of multiple subjectivities is precisely not political enough, in so far as it silently presupposes a non-thematized, 'naturalized' framework of economic relations.
>
> (*CHU*: 108)

In other words, for Žižek, the new identity politics succeeds only at the expense of itself. It operates within the parameters of capitalism but does not seek to challenge them, thereby missing what should be the real target of politics. As an example, Žižek cites studies of illegal aliens working on American farms which conclude that economic exploitation is a result of racial intolerance. By so doing, studies such as these and identity politics generally, mystify the real reasons for exploitation around the world which, Žižek argues, is actually a characteristic of capitalism.

THE RETROACTIVE ŽIŽEK

As will hopefully be clear by now, Žižek has his fingers in many pies. The limitations on his influence effected by his Lacanianism are offset by the philosophical and Marxist elements of his theories. His work, like that of many of his contemporaries, transcends the boundaries of a single discipline and therefore finds a broad constituency. That Žižek's constituency is broader than most is also because his work transcends the confines of a single subject matter. For example, while he has been generally more influential in film studies – 'Žižek's work', according to Colin McCabe, the former Head of Research at the British Film Institute, 'could be taken as the exemplar for a project of renewing the study of cinema by intensifying its theoretical ambition' (*TFRT*: viii) – his recent books have also found him a place on many religious studies courses. And although he has not always been warmly received in the field of Anglo-American philosophy, he has, with no small irony, become a staple on cultural studies programmes.

This is an irony not least because of Žižek's continued disavowal of cultural studies and because, primarily, he considers himself a philosopher. However, Žižek has helped to reinvigorate the field of philosophy precisely by referencing a wide range of popular cultural products. Indeed, it could be argued that Žižek *is* a popular cultural product. He writes with a loose-limbed and easily identifiable style that eschews the more prolix and dense associative writing of much contemporary philosophy. He releases books more regularly than Madonna releases singles. He cuts from one subject to another more readily than the average pop video cuts from one camera angle to another. And he is an icon of iconoclasm. In other words, Žižek is an 'MTV philosopher', in the sense in which the Canadian critic Clint Burnham describes Jameson as an 'MTV Marxist':

Many intellectuals of my generation read the work of Jameson, and theory in general . . . as mass culture; by my generation I suppose I mean those born in the late fifties or sixties . . . in this milieu, Jameson and Butler and Spivak and Barthes are on the same plane as Shabba Ranks and PJ Harvey and *Deep Space Nine* and John Woo: cultural signifiers of which one is as much a 'fan' as a 'critic', driven as much by the need to own or see or read the 'latest' (or the 'classic' or the 'original') as by the need to debate it on Internet or in the seminar room.

(Burnham 1995: 244)

Whereas, I would suggest, Jameson and the other theorists mentioned by Burnham are only accidentally cultural products consumed by 'theory junkies' (Burnham 1995: 243), Žižek's work largely seems to be directly targeted at such junkies, if only because he is one himself. Žižek's contemporaries are, then, we might say, younger than he is. He appeals more obviously to the next generation of theorists and therefore his influence is likely to grow with them.

The impact of Žižek on critical theory will thus be felt retroactively. But we will also 'return' to him in a much more fundamental way, the same way as he 'returns' to Lacan, and Lacan 'returns' to Freud. Which is to say that there is not simply a point 'after Žižek' when we will be able to declare that *this* is what Žižek means and *this* has been his impact. For Žižek, meaning is constantly liable to revisionism. This is not just a question of weighing up relative interpretations of his work but of having that work radically altered by the 'act', the 'night of the world' which utterly alters the horizon of its reception. The meaning, impact and influence of his work is, in this sense, traumatic. Just as the scene of his parents having intercourse only made sense to the Wolf-Man after he had developed his own sexual theories, so will our understanding of Žižek's theories change retroactively. Quite simply, Žižek will have been.

FURTHER READING

This is a list of books available in English either written, co-written, edited or co-edited by Slavoj Žižek.

WORKS AUTHORED BY SLAVOJ ŽIŽEK

Žižek, S. (1989) *The Sublime Object of Ideology*, London and New York: Verso.

This is Žižek's first major work in English and to my mind it remains one of his most accessible books. Mixing philosophy, politics and psychoanalysis with examples from high and low culture, he sets out in clear, explanatory detail his understanding of Hegel's dialectic, the basic thesis that underpins all his analyses, and one which finds that contradiction is an internal condition of every identity. Central to this enterprise is the examination of the theory which Žižek returns to time and again – that the subject is the subject of a void. If you only read one of Žižek's books then this should be it as it contains a basic explanation of almost all the key Žižekian motifs.

Žižek, S. (1991) *Looking Awry: An Introduction to Jacques Lacan through Popular Culture*, Cambridge, Massachusetts and London: MIT Press.

This text is often cited as the easiest of Žižek's books to navigate, a reputation underscored by the many and varied references to popular culture he makes throughout the text. However, as Žižek admits, this book should probably be subtitled 'Everything He Wasn't Able to Put into *The Sublime Object*'. Therefore, unless you already understand the Lacanian concepts of the Real and *jouissance* (the two aspects of Lacan's work upon which he concentrates here), then some of the analyses will seem unnecessarily foreshortened. If, on the other hand, you read *The Sublime Object of Ideology* first, you will be better able to grasp the subtleties of his arguments concerning detective fiction, pornography, democracy and Hitchcock.

Žižek, S. (1991) *For They Know Not What They Do: Enjoyment as a Political Factor*, London and New York: Verso.

Presented as a sequel to *The Sublime Object of Ideology*, this book examines the historical change emblematized by the shift in the telling of the Rabinovitch joke from that first book. In particular, it analyses the re-emergence of militant nationalism and racism in the wake of the break-up of the socialist countries of Eastern Europe. Žižek identifies the cause of this re-emergence in an eruption of enjoyment. This book also contains an extended discussion of the concept of the vanishing mediator.

Žižek, S. (1992) *Enjoy Your Symptom! Jacques Lacan In Hollywood and Out*, London and New York: Routledge.

Picking up on one of the themes of *For They Know Not What They Do*, Žižek here attends to the ideology of cynicism – the fetishist 'I know very well . . . but all the same . . .' formulation which is one of the mainstays of his work. The book is structured around five chapters, each of which endeavours to explain a fundamental Lacanian concept – letter, woman, repetition, phallus and father. Hollywood is once again the lure in this text as Žižek elaborates each concept with reference to popular culture. However, as with *Looking Awry*, the familiarity of the examples does not necessarily make this the most accessible of his books to read.

Žižek, S. (1993) *Tarrying with the Negative: Kant, Hegel and the Critique of Ideology*, Durham: Duke University Press.

This is probably Žižek's lengthiest consideration of the radical negative gesture which he consistently identifies as the hallmark of 'true' philosophy. Here he sets out the case that Lacan is the third philosopher to accomplish this gesture after Plato and Kant, both of whom also trumped the relativistic attitudes of their day by way of an act of even greater radicalization. While this may be the larger picture of the book, and part of his project as a whole, Žižek also produces his most sustained explanation of Hegel's philosophy here, as well as dissecting the *cogito*. As this synopsis suggests, *Tarrying with the Negative* is, at times, a difficult book but one which repays the effort of your labour.

Žižek, S. (1994) *The Metastases of Enjoyment: Six Essays on Woman and Causality*, London and New York: Verso.

This is one of Žižek's most rewarding books as it covers a range of crucial topics from the cause of the subject through the role of the super-ego to the impossibility of the sexual relationship. In each of the six essays, Žižek begins by asking (and ultimately answering) the kind of basic questions that anyone interested in Lacanian psychoanalysis sooner or later wants to know the answers to. In the spirit of this fundamental questioning, the book's Appendix contains a self-interview in which Žižek poses to himself the kind of queries that bother what he terms 'common knowledge' about Lacanian theory as well as his own work. As a form of self-interrogation is the elementary procedure of all his books, this interview represents Žižek in his essence or, as he might put it (in Hegelese), Žižek in the mode of 'in-itself'.

Žižek, S. (1996) *The Indivisible Remainder: An Essay on Schelling and Related Matters*, London and New York: Verso.

This book forms part of a larger project for Žižek to reinvigorate the reputation of German Idealism which, for him, constitutes the bedrock of all philosophy. His particular hope with this monograph is that he enhances the perception of Schelling's *Ages of the World* as 'one of the seminal works of materialism', divining in it a forerunner to the works of Marx and Lacan among others. The first part of the book endeavours to explain the *Ages of the World*, while the second part compares the reception of Schelling's work with the reception of Hegel's work using Lacan as the key to both. As can be imagined from this brief description, the first two parts of this volume make a complex and demanding read. The third part of the book (the 'related matters' of the title) is only relatively more accessible, but contains interesting discussions of both cyberspace and quantum physics which prefigure some of Žižek's later work.

Žižek, S. (1997) *The Plague of Fantasies*, London and New York: Verso.

This is an extended explanation of the psychoanalytical concept of fantasy. The 'plague' of the title refers to the deluge of pseudo-concrete images which Žižek places in an antagonistic relationship to the ever greater abstractions which determine our lives. As part of this discussion, Žižek advances one of his most considered analyses of cyberspace which, he avows, threatens to abolish the dimension of Symbolic virtuality. Given that fantasy plays such a key role in Žižek's anatomy of the human condition, the first chapter here – which is a seven-point clarification of the concept – is a particularly valuable addition to the Žižekian corpus, making this one of the books most suited to a first-time Žižek reader. As an added enticement, this work also contains Žižek's famous Hegelian analysis of German, French and English toilet designs.

Žižek, S. (1999) *The Ticklish Subject: The Absent Centre of Political Ontology*, London and New York: Verso.

Hailed by some critics as Žižek's most important work to date, it is – judging by the number of articles it has spawned – certainly one of his most comprehensive monographs. Its central thesis is that the 'nursery tale' of the *cogito* which has dominated modern thought (in its guise as the self-transparent thinking subject) is, in fact, a misnomer that fails to acknowledge the *cogito*'s constitutive moment of madness. Structured in three parts, the book takes to task critics of Cartesian subjectivity in the fields of German Idealism, French political philosophy and Anglo-American cultural studies, directing blame for contemporary scientific and technological catastrophes away from the *cogito* and laying it squarely at the door of capitalism. While the overall philosophical argument is enjoyable in itself, Žižek also delivers a series of fascinating local insights which range across all aspects of political, cultural and social life. While parts of the book are very demanding – and to that end I would not recommend it to a first-time Žižek reader – it does reward your patience.

Žižek, S. (2000) *The Fragile Absolute, or Why the Christian Legacy is Worth Fighting For*, London and New York: Verso.

As Žižek himself confesses, it might seem strange for a Marxist to defend the legacy of Christianity in an age which has seen the re-emergence of obscurantist religious thought. However, part of the broad remit of this compact book is an attempt to resuscitate the subversive core of Christianity, the act of 'shooting at oneself' (or of radical negativity) which forms the centrepiece of Žižek's analysis of Schelling in *The Abyss of Freedom* and of Descartes in *Cogito and the Unconscious*. Proposing that the only way to liberate oneself from the grip of existing social reality is to renounce the fantasmatic supplement that attaches us to it, he cites any number of examples from Sethe's act of infanticide in Toni Morrison's *Beloved*, through Keyser Soeze's massacre of his own family in *The Usual Suspects*, up to the supreme instance of such a gesture in the Crucifixion. This is an accessible work which underscores the utopian aspect of his discussion of the 'night of the world' in previous books.

Žižek, S. (2000) *The Art of the Ridiculous Sublime: On David Lynch's* Lost Highway, Seattle: Walter Chapin Simpson Center for the Humanities.

Using some of the material from *The Fragile Absolute*, while building on previous analyses in *The Metastases of Enjoyment* and elsewhere, this small book/essay is an examination of David Lynch's film *Lost Highway*. Amid the many satisfying incidental discussions, Žižek's central contention is that *Lost Highway* effectively functions as a form of meta-commentary on the opposition between the classic and postmodern *noir femme fatale*.

Žižek, S. (2000) *Enjoy Your Symptom! Jacques Lacan In Hollywood and Out*, 2nd edition, London and New York: Routledge.

This is exactly the same as the first edition of the book apart from an added chapter on the concept of reality. Using the film *The Matrix* as an example, Žižek looks at the relationship between the Symbolic and the Real and explains why the big Other does not exist.

Žižek, S. (2000) *The Spectre is Still Roaming Around*, Zagreb: Arkzin.

Written as the introduction to a 150th commemorative edition of Marx's *The Communist Manifesto*, this small book/essay is now sold separately. Much of the material here is a recapitulation of the ideas in the last chapter of *The Ticklish Subject*; however, Žižek structures it around a consideration of the value of *The Communist Manifesto* for us today. He argues that, despite its revolutionary shortcomings, the *Manifesto*'s analyses of the destructive effects of capital are more applicable to the world of late capitalism – a world in which the brutal imposition of a unified global market threatens all local ethnic traditions, including the very form of the Nation-State – than they ever were when it was originally written.

Žižek, S. (2000) *NATO as the Left Hand of God*, Zagreb: Arkzin.

As with *The Spectre is Still Roaming Around*, this is a small book/essay which was originally sold only in very limited editions. It focuses on Žižek's critique of the NATO bombing of former Yugoslavia. According to him, this action dramatized a false alternative between the New World Order and the neo-racist nationalists opposing it. For Žižek, on the other hand, these are the two sides of the same coin – the New World Order, in which NATO is the military arm of multi-national capitalism, itself breeds the monstrosities, such as Slobodan Milosevic, that it fights.

Žižek, S. (2001) *Did Somebody Say Totalitarianism? Five Essays in the (Mis)Use of a Notion*, London and New York: Verso.

This timely and combative book argues that totalitarianism is an ideological notion which has been used by the liberal democratic consensus to impugn the political left's critique of that consensus with the atrocities of the political right, thereby disabling effective political thought. Žižek examines five aspects of totalitarianism here and concludes that the problem with the notion is the very thing that makes such a designation possible in the first place – the liberal democratic consensus (among whose members he includes just about everybody, damning them as a bunch of 'conformist scoundrels'). Like many of his recent books, this monograph is more explicitly political in its content, ending as it does with the refrain for increased socialization 'in some form or another'.

Žižek, S. (2001) *The Fright of Real Tears: Krzysztof Kieślowski between Theory and Post-theory*, London and Bloomington: British Film Institute and Indiana University Press.

This book is an intervention in the on-going debate in the field of film studies which is split between Theory (anything loosely affiliated with structuralism and post-structuralism) and Post-Theory (anything loosely affiliated with a dislike of structuralism and post-structuralism). The main cause of antipathy for the Post-Theorists was the dominance of certain Lacanian concepts in the field of film studies. Žižek's argument here, via a reading of Krzysztof Kieślowski's films, is that these Lacanian concepts were employed piecemeal without either due regard for their philosophical matrix or for their implications. This book finds Žižek at his most robust and methodical, as he debunks the lamentable conclusions of Post-Theory, as well as at his most patient, as he explains the workings and value of Lacan's insights.

Žižek, S. (2001) *On Belief*, London and New York: Routledge.

Žižek returns here to the territory of *The Fragile Absolute* in what he describes as a 'self-critical' mood. Although advertised as an analysis of belief, the main thrust of the book is once again the call for a politics of the ethical act, one which rejects the comforts of pragmatism and repeats the hard-line and unrepentant ethic of St Paul and Lenin. As such this represents the latest of Žižek's entreaties for us to leap into the 'night of the world'. Probably his most accessible monograph to date (as well as one of his best-selling), this book can be profitably read with little prior knowledge of the rest of his work.

WORKS CO-AUTHORED BY SLAVOJ ŽIŽEK

Žižek, S. and von Schelling, F.W.J. (1975) *The Abyss of Freedom – Ages of the World*, Michigan: University of Michigan Press.

Reprising much of the material from the first part of *The Indivisible Remainder*, this book combines Žižek's essay on Schelling's *Ages of the World* with the first ever English translation of the second draft of that title. Žižek argues that at the centre of the *Ages of the World* is the struggle to resolve the enigma of sufficient reason. While most philosophers attempt to explain freedom, Schelling reverses the terms of the question and asks how we emerged from a state of freedom and became caught in a network of reason. Žižek's analysis of the answer to this question is often difficult (as is Schelling's deceptively simple prose), but is, nevertheless, recognizably cognate with the discussions of Hegel and Lacan that he undertakes in other monographs.

Žižek, S., Butler, J. and Laclau, E. (2000) *Contingency, Hegemony, Universality: Contemporary Dialogues on the Left*, London and New York: Verso.

This vigorous, pithy and hugely enjoyable work brings Žižek together with his two most assiduous intellectual sparring partners – Judith Butler and Ernesto Laclau – in a kind of written dialogue. This dialogue takes the form of a series of questions set by each of them for the others, followed by three essayed responses apiece. The main point of contention between them is the status and meaning of the subject. While, for a Žižekian, Butler's consistent misreading of Lacan can sometimes be exasperating, it does at least force Žižek to articulate his understanding of the subject as clearly as possible. As such, this makes the book a useful introduction to Žižek's thought, as well as being a valuable insight to the issues currently vexing the political left.

Žižek, S. and Dolar, M. (2002) *Opera's Second Death*, London and New York: Routledge.

If Hitchcock's films are the most common source of examples in Žižek's books, Wagner's operas probably run them a close second. Picking up on this exemplary obsession and expanding his analysis of it from *Tarrying with the Negative*, Žižek here devotes half a book to the subject – the other half being Dolar's discussion of Mozart's operas. What is slightly unusual about this book is the subtle change of emphasis where, instead of using Wagnerian opera as a means to explain Lacanian theory, Žižek is more intent here on using Lacanian theory to explain Wagnerian opera. This perhaps makes the book a more relaxing read than the standard Žižekian work, as the reader is no longer fraught with the expectation that each example will have to bear the weight of a demanding Lacanian theorem.

WORKS EDITED BY SLAVOJ ŽIŽEK

Žižek, S. (ed.) (1992) *Everything You Always Wanted to Know About Lacan (But Were Afraid to Ask Hitchcock)*, London and New York: Verso.

As loyal Žižek readers will know, no Žižek book is complete without a reference to an Alfred Hitchcock film. Here, what is usually just an incidental affection for the director's work is expanded to a book-length passion. Žižek and the other authors in this volume (including Fredric Jameson and Mladen Dolar) adopt what Žižek describes as a transferential relationship towards Hitchcock, one which allows that even the smallest details of his films are meaningful. This 'meaning-fulness' extends to the fact that, for Žižek, Hitchcock's films portray the three main types of subjectivity which correspond to the three main stages of capitalism. Probably the best of the books edited by Žižek (although well over a third is actually written by him as well), this is a very entertaining and accessible mixture of film studies and psychoanalysis.

Žižek, S. (ed.) (1994) *Mapping Ideology*, London and New York: Verso.

Bringing together a host of contemporary analyses of ideology, as well as some classic texts from the recent past, this book also contains two contributions from Žižek. One of these is an edited version of Chapter 1 in *The Sublime Object of Ideology* and the other is an original essay. This essay is perhaps Žižek's most succinct and cogent exploration of the concept of ideology. His basic thesis is that ideology functions as a kind of spectre concealing the gap between the Real and the Symbolic. The value of this book (from a Žižekian point of view) is that it allows the reader to compare Žižek's thesis with Althusser's classic essay 'Ideology and Ideological State Apparatuses' – the other main theory of ideology which utilizes Lacan's work.

Žižek, S. (ed.) (1998) *Cogito and the Unconscious*, Durham: Duke University Press.

Containing three essays by Žižek, this book is essentially a defence of the *cogito* and of transcendental subjectivity generally. At the heart of Žižek's essays is his central thesis that the subject is the 'monster' which remains when we subtract subjectivity, or the wealth of self-experience, from what he terms the 'human person'. Split into three parts, the book explains the role of the *cogito* in psychoanalysis, analyses its relationship with the body, and explores contemporary critiques of the Cartesian subject. It is a rewarding read but difficult in places.

Žižek, S. (ed.) (2002) *Revolution at the Gates: Selected Writings of Lenin from 1917*, London and New York: Verso.

Continuing with his project to disinter nuggets of political wisdom from those figures who are conventionally reviled, Žižek here avers that Lenin demonstrated an admirable ability to grasp the significance of an open and contingent moment in history. As such, Lenin figures for Žižek as a vanishing mediator, one whose insights could be productively reinvigorated in an era of multinational capitalism. In terms of Žižek's work as a whole, then, this text furthers his commitment – more evident in his recent books – to find a way to build trans-national political movements and institutions strong enough to seriously constrain the unlimited rule of capital and the liberal-democratic consensus.

WORKS CO-EDITED BY SLAVOJ ŽIŽEK

Žižek, S. and Salecl, R. (eds) (1996) *Gaze and Voice as Love Objects*, Durham: Duke University Press.

This fascinating collection of essays (mainly written by Žižek's co-conspirators in the Slovenian school of Lacan) contains two contributions from Žižek. The first article discusses the gaze and the voice (and indeed just about everything else). The second article focuses on Wagner and proceeds from the basic Lacanian thesis that 'there is no sexual relationship' because there is a constitutive antagonism in the relationship between man and woman. Love is the lure or mirage which endeavours to conceal this antagonism. As these are some of Lacan's most difficult ideas to grasp, this volume (particularly Mladen Dolar's two essays) provides a very useful supplement to their discussion in Žižek's monographs.

EDITED EDITIONS OF SLAVOJ ŽIŽEK'S WORK

Wright, E. and Wright, E. (eds) (1999) *The Žižek Reader*, Oxford and Massachusetts: Blackwell.

Most of Žižek's books are readers in themselves in so far as each one exemplifies a series of key theoretical knots that are discussed in other Žižekian monographs. What this volume does is select some of Žižek's most clear and concise expressions of those knots. Taking seriously the contention that Žižek is the philosopher of the Real, *The Žižek Reader* focuses on the centrality of the concept in his work in three fields – culture, woman, and philosophy. Each of Žižek's essays (many of which are not from his monographs) is introduced by a small explanatory summary, while the volume as a whole contains not only an overview of Žižek's work but also a Preface by the man himself. This, then, is a very good representative sample of the Žižekian oeuvre.

INTERNET RESOURCES

Takemoto, Timothy, *Official Home Page of Slavoj Žižek*, http://www. mii.kurume-u.ac.jp/~leuers/zizek.htm (accessed November 2002).

This page is 'official' in so far as Žižek himself has provided a curriculum vitae, a bibliography and a series of flattering photographs. The page also offers links to a host of other sites that either deal directly with Žižek or with Lacan.

Lacanian Ink, *Žižek Bibliography*, http://www.lacan.com/biblio graphyzi.htm (accessed November 2002).

This is one of the best available bibliographies of Žižek on the internet, including references not only to his books but also to articles, many of which have links to reproductions on-line. The site also offers a brief biography of Žižek and links to interviews with him, as well as to other Lacanian thinkers.

WORKS CITED

Works by Slavoj Žižek which are cited in this book are listed in the Further Reading section.

Burnham, Clint (1995) *The Jamesonian Unconscious: The Aesthetics of Marxist Theory*, Durham and London: Duke University Press.

Derrida, Jacques (1973) *Speech and Phenomena and Other Essays on Husserl's Theory of Signs* (trans. David B. Allison), Evanston: Northwestern University Press.

Descartes, René (1968) *Discourse on Method and the Meditations* (trans. F.E. Sutcliffe), London: Penguin Books.

Dews, Peter (1995) *The Limits of Disenchantment: Essays on Contemporary European Philosophy*, London and New York: Verso.

Eagleton, Terry (1997) 'Enjoy!', *London Review of Books*, 27 November.

Gigante, Denise (1998) 'Toward a Notion of Critical Self-Creation: Slavoj Žižek and the "Vortex of Madness"', *New Literary History*, 29: 1, 153–168.

Hanlon, Christopher (2001) 'Psychoanalysis and the Post-political: An Interview with Slavoj Žižek', *New Literary History*, 32: 1, 1–21.

Homer, Sean (1995) 'Psychoanalysis, Representation, Politics: On the (Im)possibility of a Psychoanalytic Theory of Ideology?', Centre for

Psychotherapeutic Studies, University of Sheffield, http://www.shef.ac.uk/uni/academic/NQ/psysc/staff/sihomer/prp.html (accessed November 2002).

Jameson, Fredric (1988a) *The Ideologies of Theory – Essays 1971–1986: Volume 1 – Situations of Theory*, Minneapolis: University of Minnesota Press.

Jameson, Fredric (1988b) *The Ideologies of Theory – Essays 1971–1986: Volume 2 – Syntax of History*, Minneapolis: University of Minnesota Press.

Lacan, Jacques (1977) *Écrits: A Selection* (trans. Alan Sheridan), London: Routledge.

Lovink, Geert (1995) 'Japan through a Slovenian Looking Glass: Reflections of Media and Politics and Cinema.' InterCommunication 14, http://www.ntticc.or.jp/pub/ic_mag/ic014/zizek/zizek_e.html (accessed November 2002).

Marx, Karl (1976) *Capital: Volume 1* (trans. Ben Fowkes), London: Penguin/New Left Review.

Orwell, George (1949) *Nineteen Eighty-Four*, London: Penguin.

Palahniuk, Chuck (2001) *Choke*, London: Jonathan Cape.

Pascal, Blaise (1966) *Pensées* (trans. A.J. Krailsheimer), London: Penguin.

Rorty, Richard (1989) *Contingency, Irony, and Solidarity*, Cambridge: Cambridge University Press.

INDEX